BTRIPP BOOKS

BOOK REVIEWS FROM 2013

BY BRENDAN TRIPP

These reviews originally appeared on the
"BTRIPP'S BOOKS" book review blog:
http://btripp-books.livejournal.com/

Copyright © 2016 by Brendan Tripp

ISBN 978-1-57353-413-0

An Eschaton Book

Front cover photo courtesy Kenn W. Kiser via morguefile.com.
Back cover photo courtesy Sebastian Santana via morguefile.com.

PREFACE

From 1993 through 2004, I ran the *first* manifestation of Eschaton Books (now in its third revival). Initially started as a vehicle to publish my poetry, it soon became evident that the market for poetry is vanishingly small, and in 1994 we "pivoted" into being a metaphysical press.

During this time, I was largely a one-man shop, doing everything from editorial to shipping, which was a huge time commitment, and I typically worked 14 hour days, 7 days a week to keep things moving. I bring up all this here because, despite having been a life-long avid reader, during this period I had precious little time for reading, and what reading I *did* get done was largely reviewing book submissions. However, I never stopped *buying* books, which began to stack up in prodigious "to be read" piles.

When Eschaton went out of business (in a not unusual *denouement* for a small press – we had a distributor who ended up never paying us, while selling through all our stock) in 2004, I found myself with a lot of reading to catch up on, and a need to keep my writing chops sharp. So, I began to pen little reviews of what I was reading through, and post those on the web.

As the years went by, this became "a thing" that I was doing, and, for a while, I was targeting a fairly aggressive goal of getting at least 72 non-fiction books read per year. By 2015, this had resulted in my having read and reviewed 700 books over that 12-year span.

In recent years (since the upswing in print-on-demand publishing), I have had *numerous* acquaintances suggest that I put out my reviews as books. I was, at first, rather hesitant on the concept (as, after all, the material was free to read on the web), but I eventually figured that if various people thought it was a good idea, I might as well give it a shot.

While I could have started at the beginning, with the reviews from 2004, I decided that those were less representative of the whole, so opted to begin with the most recent ones.

This is the third of these collections, and the second of the two "shorter" ones (I only put up 43 reviews in 2013, and only 40 in 2014), contrasted with 72 or more I'd done in each of the preceding seven years.

A note on my review "style": I do not write classic reviews, but more a telling of my personal interaction with a particular book. This means that I talk about where and how I got the book, how it relates to other things I've read, what sort of reactions it triggered in me (and why), and how one can get a copy if it sounds appealing. Needless to say, if the reader is devoted to standard book reviewing styles, this might be an irritation ... however, it does make these reviews somewhat idiosyncratic to *me*, resulting in a collection that is something of a "my encounters with books" sort of deal, which will, hopefully, be of interest to many readers.

- Brendan Tripp

CONTENTS

v - **Preface**

vii - **Contents**

1 - Thursday, January 3, 2013

Defining the "other" ...
**Savage Anxieties:
The Invention of Western Civilization**
by Robert A. Williams, Jr.

5 - Sunday, January 20, 2013

*You keep using that word.
I do not think it means what you think it means.*
The Devil's Dictionary
by Ambrose Bierce

8 - Monday, January 21, 2013

Stories of blurred ancestry ...
A Writer's People: Ways of Looking and Feeling
by V.S. Naipaul

12 - Sunday, May 5, 2013

A new way of thinking about systems ...
Antifragile: Things that Gain from Disorder
by Nassim Nicholas Taleb

15 - Monday, May 6, 2013

Healing with the mind ...
The Hypnosis Treatment Option
by Scott D. Lewis

17 - Tuesday, May 7, 2013

"Don't be schtupid, be a schmarty ..."
**The Nazi Séance: The Strange Story
of the Jewish Psychic in Hitler's Circle**
by Arthur J. Magida

19 - Friday, May 17, 2013

Me, I'm not a fanboy ...
Think Like Zuck: The Five Business Secrets of Facebook's Improbably Brilliant CEO Mark Zuckerberg
by Ekaterina Walter

22 - Saturday, May 18, 2013

It's really what you pin ...
Pinterest Power: Market Your Business, Sell Your Product, and Build Your Brand on the World's Hottest Social Network
by Jason Miles & Karen Lacey

25 - Sunday, May 19, 2013

The Fusion Fire Hose ...
The Fusion Marketing Bible: Fuse Traditional Media, Social Media, & Digital Media to Maximize Marketing
by Lon Safko

28 - Tuesday, May 21, 2013

Dat's one speecy-spicy sundae!
Meatball Sundae: Is Your Marketing Out of Sync?
by Seth Godin

31 - Tuesday, May 21, 2013

A little review of a very bad time ...
Starting Over: Why the Last Decade Was so Damn Rotten and Why the Next One Will Surely Be Better
by Andy Serwer

33 - Saturday, May 25, 2013

Well, here's another nice Mesh ...
The Mesh: Why the Future of Business Is Sharing
by Lisa Gansky

36 - Sunday, May 26, 2013

When is a dummy not a dummy?
HTML5 For Dummies Quick Reference
by Andy Harris

38 - Wednesday, June 5, 2013

On instituting something new ..
Relentless Innovation: What Works, What Doesn't – And What That Means For Your Business
by Jeffrey Phillips

41 - Monday, June 10, 2013

Step right up ...
Life's Golden Ticket
by Brendon Burchard

44 - Friday, July 19, 2013

A how-to for growing a business ...
Let Go To Grow: Why Some Businesses Thrive and Others Fail to Reach Their Potential
by Doug and Polly White

47 - Monday, August 5, 2013

Movin' on up ...
Skyscraper Facades of the Gilded Age: Fifty-One Extravagant Designs, 1875-1910
by Joseph J. Korom, Jr.

51 - Tuesday, August 6, 2013

"Mediators of energy-matter interaction."
The Seven Wisdoms of Life: a Journey into the Chakras
by Shai Tubali

54 - Wednesday, August 7, 2013

Help Not Hype ...
Youtility: Why Smart Marketing Is about Help Not Hype
by Jay Baer

58 - Thursday, August 8, 2013

Into Tibet ...
China's Great Train: Beijing's Drive West and the Campaign to Remake Tibet
by Abrahm Lustgarten

61 - Friday, August 9, 2013

Didn't see it coming, I guess ...

**My Path Leads to Tibet:
The Inspiring Story of How One Young Blind Woman
Brought Hope to the Blind Children of Tibet**

by Sabriye Tenberken

63 - Saturday, August 10, 2013

You sometimes wonder ...

**To Live or to Perish Forever:
Two Tumultuous Years in Pakistan**

by Nicholas Schmidle

66 - Sunday, August 11, 2013

Watching others' searching ...

Exchanges Within: Questions from Everyday Life

by John Pentland

69 - Monday, August 12, 2013

Exploring the Seventh Sense ...

**The Sense of Being Stared At:
And Other Aspects of the Extended Mind**

by Rupert Sheldrake

73 - Tuesday, August 13, 2013

All over the map ...

**The Quark and the Jaguar:
Adventures in the Simple and the Complex**

by Murray Gell-Mann

76 - Saturday, August 17, 2013

Mind-Body Healing ...

**Miraculous Health: How to Heal Your Body
by Unleashing the Hidden Power of Your Mind**

by Dr. Rick Levy

79 - Sunday, August 18, 2013

Talking to the wind ...

The Alchemist

by Paulo Coelho

81 - Monday, August 19, 2013

T-T-T-Talkin' 'bout HIS generation ...
Promote Yourself: The New Rules for Career Success
by Dan Schawbel

84 - Sunday, September 1, 2013

A personal journey into cultural change ...
From the Ground Up:
A Food Grower's Education in Life, Love, and the Movement That's Changing the Nation
by Jeanne Nolan

87 - Wednesday, September 11, 2013

Sit down and shut up ...
Stop Talking, Start Communicating:
Play Dumb, Be Boring, Blow Things Off, Lose Your Friends, and Other Counterintuitive Secrets to Success in Business and in Life
by Geoffrey Tumlin

90 - Sunday, September 15, 2013

Outside of society ...
Rock & Roll Jihad: A Muslim Rock Star's Revolution
by Salman Ahmad

93 - Sunday, October 13, 2013

A question of making ...
Fabricated: The New World of 3D Printing
by Hod Lipson & Melba Kurman

96 - Monday, October 14, 2013

Revisioning marketing for the digital era ...
Marketing in the Round: How to Develop an Integrated Marketing Campaign in the Digital Era
by Gini Dietrich & Geoff Livingston

98 - Tuesday, October 15, 2013

Or do they?
QR Codes Kill Kittens:
How to Alienate Customers, Dishearten Employees, and Drive Your Business into the Ground
by Scott Stratten

100 - Tuesday, October 29, 2013

How true? How real?
Manuscript Found in Accra
by Paulo Coelho

103 - Wednesday, October 30, 2013

Speaking of which ...
The Human Voice: How This Extraordinary Instrument Reveals Essential Clues About Who We Are
by Anne Karpf

106 - Saturday, November 2, 2013

Celebrity reading ...
American on Purpose: The Improbable Adventures of an Unlikely Patriot
by Craig Ferguson

108 - Sunday, November 3, 2013

Groping towards security ...
Permanent Emergency: Inside the TSA and the Fight for the Future of American Security
by Kip Hawley & Nathan Means

111 - Monday, November 4, 2013

A man of wealth and taste ...
Dr. Faustus
by Christopher Marlow

114 - Saturday, November 9, 2013

What's not to like?
Likeable Business: Why Today's Consumers Demand More and How Leaders Can Deliver
by Dave Kerpen

117 - Sunday, November 10, 2013

No, really ... there ARE "safe nukes"!
SuperFuel: Thorium, the Green Energy Source for the Future
by Richard Martin

121 - Sunday, December 1, 2013

And in this corner ...
**Jab, Jab, Jab, Right Hook:
How to Tell Your Story in a Noisy Social World**
by Gary Vaynerchuk

124 - Saturday, December 28, 2013

Where work is heading?
Remote: Office Not Required
by Jason Fried & David Heinemeier Hansson

127 - **QR Code Links**

139 - **Contents - Alphabetical By Author**

143 - **Contents - Alphabetical By Title**

Thursday, January 3, 2013[1]

Defining the "other" ...

I got this book via the LibraryThing.com "Early Reviewers" program this Fall. I'm a bit late with the review (it took me two months from when it came it to get around to reading it), but I'm just squeaking in on the 3-month window for LTER reviews!

I think Robert A. Williams, Jr.'s Savage Anxieties: The Invention of Western Civilization[2] would have been a very useful study in another author's hands. Unfortunately, Williams is a Law professor, and this eventually plays out like a rambling legal argument in front of a jury, waiting to come in with the "payoff" at the end of this with a pitch for Native American rights (and of course, painting American culture as *racist*), his main area of activity. Frankly, it's a long way to go from the earliest awakenings of Greek civilization through the whole history of Western culture, just to make a case against the (admittedly shameful) on-going treatment of "indigenous peoples" both in the US and elsewhere. This is where the book leads:

> By now we are all too familiar with the stereotypes and imagery of a language of savagery that has been a constant part of the contemporary West's unrelenting wars against terrorism, drugs, crime, undocumented immigrants, and other enemies of civilization. ... A language of savagery has become an indispensable part of the culture, ethics, and morality of consumption throughout the West today.

Considering Williams' background in promoting tribalism, and that he has been funded by anti-American financier George Soros, it's no surprise that this is the end point of the argument. But how does he get here? From the introduction:

> From its very beginnings in ancient Greece, Western civilization has sought to invent itself through the idea of the savage. We are all familiar with the basic elements of the idea: The savage is a distant, alien, uncivilized being, unaware of either the benefits or burdens of modernity. Lacking in sophisticated institutions of government and religion, ignorant of property and laws, without complex social bonds or familial ties, living in a state of untamed nature, fierce and ennobled at the same time, the savage has always represented an anxious, negating presence in the world, standing perpetually opposed to Western civilization.

He argues that without this concept of the "savage" our civilization would never have come to be (and, by that I suppose implying that without the concept, I'd be running around Britain naked with blue tattoos like my Pictish ancestors today). Frankly, I don't find his arguments particularly convincing, as from the start he conflates a general *attitude* of superiority with material in Homer. He's certainly on base with this:

> These ... notions helped the Greeks define collectively who they were as a people and what separated and distinguished them apart from those people who inhabited the distant, uncharted parts of the world. To the ancient Greeks, the rest of the world was inhabited for the most part by tribes of savage, uncivilized "barbarians". ... "Barbarian" was an onomatopoeic term that basically translated as "babblers". It was used generally to refer to people who could not speak the Greek language or who could not speak it well.

Where is the difference in this from any regional group of people defining their ways as opposed to the ways of their neighbors? Is this much different from a Chicagoan referring to a Wisconsin resident as a "cheesehead" or the Japanese calling Koreans "garlic eaters"? He anchors his entire thesis in this, once coupled to descriptions of non-Greek peoples (or non-human monsters) in the *Iliad* and the *Odyssey*. For Homer, these flights of fantasy are in the same nature as later map makers penning "here there be monsters" on unknown parts of the world. Williams argues that this was a *racist* impulse, with these groups being "races" ... for example, the well-known mythological human/horse-hybrid Centaurs

> Centaurs were long represented in Greek mythology as mountain-dwelling, lawless, hypersexualized creatures, paradigm examples of savage beings, driven by their bestial passions and irrational urges to violate the most sacred laws of civilized humanity.

His "case" is further backed by other creatures from Homer, and how they're defeated/marginalized by the Greek "heroes", and he bases the rest of the book on this foundation. The very next thing he brings up is "colonization" of the Ionian speakers into the eastern Mediterranean ... a familiar bugaboo of non-Western cultures ... but, again, here presented as a basic function of the "racist" Greeks.

He next looks at the "golden age" myth in the works of Hesiod, and the beginning of the concept of the *noble* (non-monstrous) savage. This then works its way to the classic Greek philosophers and the development of "the West's first great imperial civilization". Like "races", and "colonization", "imperial" is another trigger word here, and Williams brings back Homer as a key defining element in the conflicts with the Persian and Scythian cultures. He takes the "savage" concept and pinballs it through a landscape of

Greek philosophical expression, and then drops the reader right into Rome. Shifting to using the architecture and sculpture of the Romans, and the writing of Caesar and others:

> *Tacitus also follows Caesar in adopting the Greeks' organizing principle of the barbarian savage's distance from Rome as determining the degree of cultural divergence from civilized norms and values.*

Again, like Homer, the Roman writers tended to "fill in the blank spots" in their writings with fantastic visions ... however, when the Roman civilization fell, and the medieval Church came to power, *"the theme of the noble savage directly contradicted the biblical story of the Fall of Adam and Eve"* and Christian redemption, and this element of the Classical world view was actively suppressed, and *"replaced by the biblically derived image of the Wild Man as an unredeemable, irrational, and forsaken enemy to the Christian message of salvation"*. The fantasized creatures of the Greeks and Romans were turned to demons by the Church, and "the savage" was linked to being in league with the devil. Rather than being those outside the cultural norm, anything outside of the lines of theological doctrine was now demonic ... providing a great impetus to the Crusades, witch hunts, etc., and giving a powerful tool to define any group unwilling to allow missionary incursions as an outright enemy of the faith.

Even into the Renaissance, this view expanded, and Pope Innocent IV's theory of "infidel rights" directed that pagan peoples *"could be lawfully conquered, colonized, and converted by Christian princes acting on authority"* of the papacy. This, of course, came in quite handy when Columbus opened up a "new world" to European expansion. I wonder how Williams missed the irony of his descriptions of Columbus' early contacts with Caribbean tribal people, whose warnings about *other* tribes are almost exactly like the "monsters" of Homer ... clearly showing that this is *not* a Western, racist, survival of a Greek attitude, but a common *human* trait to dehumanize the little-known "other"!

Oddly, the religious underpinnings of expansion and conquest were not set aside during the Renaissance. Even the English had legal justifications built up upon Christian doctrinal foundations:

> *Infidels ... were regarded at law as perpetual enemies ... of a Christian kingdom. Thus, they had no rights under English common law: "... for between them, as with devils, whose subject they be, and the Christian, there is perpetual hostility, and can be no peace."*

The difference being, of course, that this had evolved from enabling Rome to grant license to kings, to *kingdoms* (i.e. governments) being inherently enabled and encouraged to *conquer* any non-Christian peoples they encountered *"Because the way of conquering them is much more easy than of civilizing them by fair means..."*.

The Enlightenment did bring a reduction of the religious framing of this approach, but it was replaced by a "scientific" theory in which there were developmental gradations of human culture, and the more primitive would be, naturally, swept away by the more advanced. This view was very firmly established among the founding fathers of the USA, and was the basis on which interaction with the indigenous tribes proceeded, holding *"the Indian as a doomed form of human savagery"*. Further (from a Canadian legal document):

> *A civilized nation first discovering a country of uncivilized people or savages held such country as its own until such time as by treaty it was transferred to some other civilized nation. The savages' rights of sovereignty even of ownership were never recognized.*

Frankly, it has only been in the past half century that there's been any serious countering of attitudes of this nature (and even more extreme ones) towards non-Western peoples. For an example of where these attitudes might have begun to shift (allowing for a new paradigm to arise in the 60's and beyond), I'd recommend James Bradley's The Imperial Cruise[3] which traces out what happened when this sort of attitude hit Asia, and ended up inventing modern Japan (a case of "the savage" beating "the civilized" at their own game), and thus dramatically changing the world.

Again, there is a lot of very *interesting* stuff in Savage Anxieties[4], but I'm thinking the author stretches his basic thesis very thin over parts of this, all pointing to the last sections on activism for indigenous peoples. There is a taint of "Western Civilization = BAD, tribal culture = GOOD" throughout the book, which leaves a bad taste in one's mouth if one is not already on board with the message. While I think this would be far more popular with those who *are* "in the choir" that Williams is preaching to, there's enough good stuff here as a historical survey to keep up the interest of those who are otherwise convinced. This has only been out since the Fall, so I guess there's at least a chance of finding it at the more expansive brick-and-mortar book vendors, but the on-line guys have it for about a quarter off of cover price, which seems to be your best bet as not enough copies have floated down to the used channel to be at a substantially lower rate there. In conclusion, while I found this intellectually stimulating, it was also somewhat irritating, and I really wish that writing it had been done by a historian rather than an activist.

Notes:

1. http://btripp-books.livejournal.com/141247.html

2. http://amzn.to/1JSlwxn

3. http://btripp-books.livejournal.com/105712.html

4. http://amzn.to/1JSlwxn

Sunday, January 20, 2013[1]

You keep using that word. I do not think it means what you think it means.

As I've noted numerous times in the past, one of the best uses of the Dover Thrift Editions (aside from nudging an Amazon order up over $25 to get free shipping) is that I can, for a couple of bucks, fill in some hole in my education. I've been *aware* of Ambrose Bierce's The Devil's Dictionary[2] since high school, but aside from seeing the occasional quote from it, I'd never had a copy, and the last time I was looking to make shipping disappear on a book order, I opted to pick this up.

Now, as one might expect, this is a *dictionary*, so there's not much to talk about in terms of concepts, flow, etc. It starts with "A" and works its way to "Z" over something north of a thousand words. Although he was a reasonably prolific writer, The Devil's Dictionary[3] is probably Bierce's best-known work to the general reader. This is perhaps due to his life and career paralleling that of Samuel Clemens (Mark Twain), who was by far the more famous of the two. Bierce was also more of a critic, and was known to indulge in bitter/biting prose rather that humor of Twain. Unlike Twain (who had headed West to avoid the unpleasantries of the Civil War) Bierce was a military man, having served half a decade in the Union army. He is presumed to have died in the pursuit of a story, having gone down to Mexico in the middle of their revolution, where he simply disappeared.

Since this is just a collection of definitions (albeit rather arch takes on things), I figured the best way to represent the book here would be to excerpt the bits that seemed most appealing to me. I am taking the liberty of shortening some of these, and omitting the questionable poetry (variously and, I'm sure, spuriously attributed to fictional names) that accompanies some of these So ...

> **Abrupt,** *adj.* Sudden, without ceremony, like the arrival of a cannon-shot and the departure of the soldier whose interests are most effected by it.
>
> **Abscond,** *v.i.* To "move in a mysterious way," commonly with the property of another.
>
> **Cannon,** *n.* An instrument employed in the rectification of national boundaries.
>
> **Connoisseur,** *n.* A specialist who knows everything about something and nothing about anything else.
>
> **Consul,** *n.* In American politics, a person who having failed to secure an office from the people is giv-

en one by the Administration on condition that he leave the country.

Diaphragm, *n.* A muscular partition separating disorders of the chest from disorders of the bowels.

Dictator, *n.* The chief of a nation that prefers the pestilence of despotism to he plague of anarchy.

Diplomacy, *n.* The patriotic art of lying for one's country.

Fidelity, *n.* A virtue peculiar to those who are about to be betrayed.

Hand, *n.* A singular instrument worn at the end of a human arm and commonly thrust into somebody's pocket

Happiness, *n.* An agreeable sensation arising from contemplating the misery of another.

Hearse, *n.* Death's baby-carriage.

Heathen, *n.* A benighted creature who has the folly to worship something that he can see and feel.

Mammon, *n.* The god of the world's leading religion. His chief temple is in the holy city of New York.

Mayonnaise, *n.* One of the sauces which serve the French in place of a state religion.

Mind, *n.* A mysterious form of matter secreted by the brain. Its chief activity consists in the endeavor to ascertain its own nature, the futility of the attempt being due to the fact that it has nothing but itself to know itself with.

Piety, *n.* Reverence for the Supreme Being, based upon His supposed resemblance to man.

> *The pig is taught by sermons and epistles*
> *To think the God of Swine has snout and bristles.*
>
> *Judibras.*

Politeness, *n.* The most acceptable hypocrisy.

Pray, *v.* To ask that the laws of the universe be annulled in behalf of a single petitioner confessedly unworthy.

Prescription, *n.* A physician's guess at what will best prolong the situation with least harm to the patient.

Saint, *n.* A dead sinner revised and edited.

> **Take,** *v.t.* To acquire, frequently by force but preferably by stealth.
>
> **Un-American,** *adj.* Wicked, intolerable, heathenish.
>
> **Zeal,** *n.* A certain nervous disorder afflicting the young and inexperienced.

As noted, a good number of the "definitions" here are accompanied with poems, some as long as 50-60 lines. I suspect that these might be lampooning events and characters from the time of the individual entry's composition (this was serialized in weekly publications over the rather remarkably long run of twenty-five years, from 1881 to 1906), as the poems are only round-about illustrations of the associated words, with odd details, and unusual names or initials for their attributions. I'm guessing that there are "annotated" versions of this out there which pick some of that apart.

The Devil's Dictionary[4] is widely available, with the Dover edition being a mere $3.50, but (given its vintage) I'm pretty sure you'll be able to find it free on-line somewhere. Obviously, "reading a dictionary" is not something that appeals to everybody (some folks demand *plot* and stuff), but this is an amusing read, and despite being rather slim (this printing comes to 144 pages), it might be a great thing for one's latrine library!

Notes:

1. http://btripp-books.livejournal.com/141529.html
2-4. http://amzn.to/1PZzIWH

Monday, January 21, 2013[1]

Stories of blurred ancestry ...

As regular followers of this space know, I don't read very much fiction ... I used to, but haven't "gone there" much over most of the past decade. I bring this up not to introduce what would be a *very* rare fiction review, but to note that the author of this volume is best known for his novels, and is the recipient of a dozen or so literary awards, up to and including a Nobel Prize in Literature. This book, however is something of an auto-biographical journey through authors he has read at various points in his life, and how they influenced him along the way.

Again, regular readers of my reviews might be thinking *"gee, this isn't the stuff Brendan usually gets into ... what's up with it?"*, well, this is another example of leveraging the dollar store to expand the range of what I'm reading. I'd run across V.S. Naipaul's A Writer's People: Ways of Looking and Feeling[2] a couple of months back, and jumped into it as a change of pace.

Naipaul has a rather convoluted biography, but one that's not too odd for coming along at the last gasps of the British Empire. His family was from India, but was living in Trinidad when he was born. He moved to England to attend college and began his career as a writer. This book takes a look at five writers whose careers or writings influenced his, in one way or another. There is Caribbean poet Derek Walcott, British novelist Anthony Powell, an Indian who had emigrated to the Dutch South American colony of Surinam, Rahman Khan, French novelist Gustave Flaubert (of *Madame Bovary* fame), whose chapter somehow dovetails into a discussion of Julius Caesar's *The Gallic War*, and finally to Indian author Nirad Chaudhuri.

Each of these writers had something that spoke to Naipaul, as he tried to fit his experience into the wider world, trying to fit his "Indian-ness" into a world that was no longer defined by the reach of Britannia, and how he, as a colonial product, fit in England, and into an evolving new (post-war) global reality that was far less defined than it had been a generation before. Naipaul was born in 1932, and did not go to London until after WW2, entering Oxford on a scholarship in 1950. The authors he discusses here each have a piece to the puzzle which he is trying to make sense of, from being a voice from the colonies, to being an observer of a dramatically changing world, to a witness to a personal cultural exodus, to the textures of civilization, and eventually to the great changes in India wrought by Gandhi and his contemporaries.

Naipaul weaves in and out through these chapters between biographical material, historical context, media scuttlebutt, literary criticism, and his own personal reflections. These latter elements are, of course, the core here, and are, ultimately, what A Writer's People[3] hinges on. Here's a bit from his discussion of Walcott:

> It was something we with literary ambitions from these islands all had to face: small places with simple economies bred small people with simple destinies. And these islands were very small, infinitely smaller than Ibsen's Norway. Their literary possibilities, like their economic possibilities, were as narrow as their human possibilities. Ibsen's Norway, provincial as it was, had bankers, editors, scholars, high-reaching people. There was nothing of this human wealth in the islands. They didn't give a fiction-writer or a poet much to write about; they cramped and quickly exhausted a talent which in a larger and more varied space might have spread its wings and done unsuspected things.
>
> It was a literary blight that in varying ways affected other places as well: big countries that for political or other reasons had become hard to write about as they were. So Camus in the 1940s could cleanse Algeria of Arabs; and twenty or thirty years later some South African writers, fatigued by the theme of race, with its inevitabilities, its pressures to do the right thing, could seek to create a race-free no man's land to give room to their private imaginings.

There are few straight paths here ... the narrative meanders through back alleys and tea rooms, across continents. The author turns his contacts and influences over and inside out to see what they're about and then reflects on what they mean, and what they mean to him. In the intro to the chapter about his early career in London, he notes:

> I grew up on an island like Walcott's. Other races were close, but for my first five or six years, in the 1930s, I lived in a transplanted peasant India. This India was being washed away by the stringencies of our colonial life, but it still felt whole, and this gave me a base of feeling and cultural knowledge which even members of my family who came later didn't have. This base of feeling has lasted all my life. I think it is true to say that, in the beginning, living in this unusual India, I saw people of other groups but at the same time didn't see them. This made me receptive to my father's stories of a self-contained local Indian life and the healing power of Indian ritual. I was more than receptive to these stories; I was greatly moved by them. I saw them being written and was dazzled by them.

One thing to point out here was that not only his father, but a number of his relatives were authors, so writing, and the written word were things close to Naipaul's personal identity (perhaps explaining the support of his law-student cousin in his early years of writing in London – where many other families would have been screaming for him to enter commerce!). But the concept, if not the sub-continent, of India hovers over much of the book, in people's actions, perceptions, and realities.

> Little by little the India of myth was chipped away, and India became a place of destitution from which we were lucky to have got away. I went myself when I was twenty-nine. I went from England; at that time I was eleven years out of Trinidad. And still I went to that second India, the India from which we had to get away and not to the India of independence and the great names of the independence movement. I went with jangling nerves, which became worse the closer the ship got to Bombay.

The look at Flaubert, Caesar, and Virgil, is a bit harder to fit to the general arc of [A Writer's People](#)[4] as it deals more with literary criticism, the *technology* of the writing, if you will. Naipaul contrasts the composition of *Madame Bovary* with the far more florid and detailed *Salammbo*, and considers the classical sources of the latter's story … but this exists more as an academic exercise rather than his own self-searching:

> Ambition makes a writer reach beyond what he has already achieved. And this is when, out of his security, he can make misjudgements. This misjudgement might have to do with something small, so as a matter of style, a way of writing that has crept up on a writer. Sometimes it is more serious, the very conception of a book. The more the writer feels ill at ease, the harder he tries, using all the resources of his talent, to prove his point; and then, seeing him suffer to do so, one is more than half in sympathy with him.

I wonder if the author is wondering if he's successfully maintaining *his* aim here, as this part of the book seems to drift far afield, except as a look a how one can mine research and lose one's authenticity. To risk making too much of a drift myself here, I did want to make a note on a detail that he references that I found fascinating, as it plays into the Gurdjieff teachings: "'The souls of the dead,' he said, 'are dissolved in the moon as corpses are in the earth. Their tears provide its moisture; it is a dark place full of mud, ruins, and storms…'", this in a quotation that he describes as arising from "bad nineteenth-century fiction, gothic, orientalist …", which makes me wonder how the two might have been connected (if at all).

A Writer's People[5] does not come to a solid conclusion, but ends with some statements:

> India remains hidden. Indian writers, to speak generally, seem to know only about their own families and their places of work. It is the Indian way of living and consequently the Indian way of seeing. The rest of the country is taken for granted and seen superficially ...
>
> India has no means of judging, India is hard and materialist. What it knows best about Indian writers and books are their advances and their prizes. There is little discussion about the substance of a book or its literary quality or the point of view of the writer. ...
>
> India's poverty and colonial past, the riddle of the two civilizations, continue to stand in the way of identity and strength and intellectual growth.

This is a very richly written book, which engages the reader in its bits and pieces, but lacks an overall feeling as a whole. It is fascinating in its details, but feels more like a collection of disparate parts. It is still in print, and can be ordered from the on-line big boys for its full cover price, but since it had run through the dollar store channel, you can find *new* copies via the new/used guys for as little as 14¢ (plus shipping), and you might still be able to find it at the Dollar Tree stores for a buck. I enjoyed reading this but it's probably most appealing to those with an interest in Indian culture, the decline of the British Empire, and the various literary threads that run through it.

Notes:

1. http://btripp-books.livejournal.com/141754.html
2-5. http://amzn.to/1PZz4bT

Sunday, May 5, 2013[1]

A new way of thinking about systems ...

Wow ... it's been *months* since I've been able to block the time out to get over to the coffee shop (for some reason, I can't write at home) to knock out some reviews! Frankly, I'm "late" with this one ... I won this in the LibraryThing-.com "Early Reviewers" program, from the September 2012 batch, and it did not get into my hands until late December. Officially, we're supposed to have a review in within 3 months, and it's been four and a half. Maybe they'll cut me some slack with this being a 500-page tome of fairly obscure stuff.

I'd not been aware of Nassim Nicholas Taleb's work previously, but he does seem to be particularly noted for his "Black Swan" work (not the movie) on high-impact yet rare events. His field of study deals with "uncertainty, probability, and knowledge" and this book, Antifragile: Things that Gain from Disorder[2] is part of a loose trilogy of books in that arena.

Frankly, the concept of something that is "antifragile" is somewhat difficult to grasp ... it's part of a triad of states, the other two of which are common: *fragile* and *robust*. Taleb had been a trader, and a good deal of what he bases the material here on is phrased in rather technical language from the study of volatility, with "gamma" and "vega" and other mathematical concepts that went right over my head. Early in the book he has a table with dozens of examples these states as expressed in different realms, but I'm hard pressed to pull examples to give you a clear idea of these categories because, in many of them, one of the three is missing, and in a *lot* of them, the example he gives requires a trip to the glossary! One is pretty straightforward: Business. In this "Industry" is fragile, "Small Business" is robust, and being an "Artisan" is *antifragile*. For "Literature" he has e-readers as fragile, books as robust, and oral tradition as antifragile ... for Science he has theory as fragile, phenomenology as robust, and heuristics as antifragile.

Speaking of science, Taleb has a rather charming concept which he calls the "Soviet-Harvard Illusion" which shines a wholly unflattering light on both government and academia (and the media for good measure as a contributing factor):

> The Soviet-Harvard illusion (i.e., lecturing birds on flying and believing in being the cause behind these wonderful skills) belongs to a class of causal illusions called epiphenomena. What are these illusions? ...
>
> An epiphenomena is when you don't observe A without observing B with it, so you are likely to think that A causes B, or that B causes A, depending on

> the cultural framework or what seems plausible to the local journalist. ...
>
> The narrative fallacy is a more general disease of always wanting narratives instead of disconnected facts, or facts not glued by cause and effects. That's how our minds work and that's the prime reason I hate the media because it exploits our mental defects and gives us the illusion that more things on Planet Earth are explainable than they really are, hence more predictable.

Just about the only government (or large institution) that Taleb has any admiration for is Switzerland, of which he says: *Note for now that this is the last major country that is not a nation-state, but rather a collection of small municipalities left to their own devices.* In general the large is fragile, while the small and specialized is robust, and the small and *unspecialized* is "antifragile".

Another concept that he introduces here is "iatrogenics" (which I'd not previously encountered), which means "caused by the healer", and can be generalized to any form of interventionism (such as Congress passing *horrible* laws in response to particular and fleeting events that cause untold harm in their on-going application). This can, and does, crop up in endless institutional settings, from the clamor in the press for "something to be done", to regulation for the sake of regulation, to examples of surgeries that become ubiquitous because they are both profitable and easy to prescribe.

Taleb has stories in here based on characters introduced in his previous books, including "Fat Tony" who has made his life's fortune in "not being a sucker", and illustrates how he "bets" against the sucker response ... costing him small amounts on-going, but paying off massively when the suckers all make a move (which is interestingly also paralleled in a story of Greek philosopher Thales of Miletus, who, having been challenged to, essentially, "put his money where his mouth is", created the first "option" deal on record, paying all the olive-press owners in the area a small amount to have rights to use their presses preferentially at some time in the future, having accurately predicted a large harvest that season). Much like the "sucker/non-sucker" dichotomy, there's also the "turkey/non-turkey" split. This story is based on the trust the turkey has for the farmer ... it goes a thousand days being well fed and cared for ... until the day the axe comes out. This concept also comes up in showing fragility vs. antifragility in careers, with the story of two brothers, one of whom is a corporate executive, living a life with much of the variability smoothed out, and another who is a taxi driver whose days are up and down, but always providing actionable feedback, and averaging out over time. One day the first brother is downsized (like the turkey), and faced with dire prospects, while (barring truly extreme occurrences) the second brother can weather most conditions that come his way.

Antifragile[3] is not an easy read, on several levels. As noted above, it does veer off into technical aspects of some fairly obscure arenas, and Taleb introduces very unusual terms, perhaps defining them initially, but subsequently as a basic element (the word *flâneur* is one that had me flipping back to the glossary on several occasions) ... making me wish that the Glossary (which is a fascinating read in itself) had appeared at the *front* of the book. Taleb is also unwilling to suffer either fools or those he considers frauds (and worse), and seems to have little compunction on calling them out, by name, with a good deal of venom (even to the point of coining various "Ethical Problems" with some of the more notable miscreants' names). It was also, to my reading, not particularly *linear*, floating in and out of historical, economic, political, academic, and street realms, with not much of a discernible "arc". Frankly, I kept hoping that he'd detail Fat Tony's secrets, but if they're in there, they're in a meta level that I must not have connected enough of the dots to get!

I have an ARC (advanced reading copy) of this, so can't speak to the final version, but it's relatively new (publication date last November), and the online big boys have it at nearly half off at the moment. If you're interested in a challenging book that will get you to think about stuff that you have likely not thought much about, I'd say give it a go ... but with the above caveats on it not being an *easy* read.

Notes:

1. http://btripp-books.livejournal.com/141931.html

2-3. http://amzn.to/1iaYXLu

Monday, May 6, 2013[1]

Healing with the mind ...

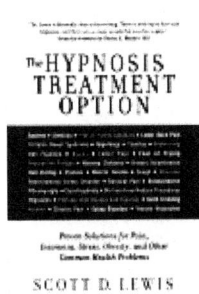

This is another book that came my way via the "Early Reviewer" program at LibraryThing.com ... in this case from the December 2012 "batch". As I've noted previously, this lends a certain serendipity to my reading, as I get books from there pretty close to monthly and they typically are ones that I might not have picked up or ordered if they weren't being offered by LTER. A number of years ago I took a hypnosis training course, and have read a number of books on the subject, so it was fairly logical that I'd have been selected (check out this FAQ[2] for details on how LTER works) to get Scott D. Lewis' The Hypnosis Treatment Option[3].

Dr. Lewis has an interesting bio, having been a Chiropractor who was frustrated in helping his over-weight patients in his Las Vegas practice, and had felt somewhat hypocritical in his efforts as he was rather overweight himself. One day he got a mailing about a hypnosis training program for medical professionals, signed up, and found that the tools he got from hypnosis helped him to take off the extra pounds, keep them off, and begin to help his patients with their weight struggles. Evidently hypnosis was appealing to him, as he eventually ended up doing a long-running "comedy hypnosis" show at the Riviera Hotel!

This book, however, is serious to a fault. One gets the sense that Dr. Lewis is seeking to step away from the showy elements of hypnosis and build a groundwork for more serious, medical, usages. There is an feeling of him being somewhat defensive here, as though he needs to support hypnosis as a practice ... largely expressed by his extensive use of reference footnotes to hundreds of studies. Unfortunately, his reliance on this research material (while frequently *fascinating* in what it reveals), and tone that comes close to "apologetics", creates a work which is almost not for the general reader.

The book is in three sections, the first part being about hypnosis in general, with descriptions of the practice, its history, discussions of myths about it, instructions for finding qualified hypnotists, and an outline of self-hypnosis techniques. This takes up about a quarter of the book, and was, to me, the most useful portion. The second part is a look at hypnosis being used in the treatment of a number of conditions, with chapters dedicated to fourteen common ailments, ranging from headaches to weight loss, to stress management. Each of these chapters has a discussion of the malady, a look at how hypnosis can help, a look at how this works for children (where applicable), a case study, and how hypnosis might have advantages over other treatments. The third section is very short, with a listing (with a few paragraphs each) of another 33 illnesses that hypnosis can help with, and an Epilog, Glossary, and Resource listing.

Frankly, reading through the second and third sections got a little tiring ... I'm not a doctor, and I really don't care so much about conditions I don't have ... which is *most* of what's in there (thankfully). Again, this is where I was getting the "not for the general reader" sense about the book, as a healthcare provider (or dedicated hypochondriac) might find this listing of sickness after sickness interesting, it was a bit much to slog through.

What *was* interesting, however, were the statistics he cites for success rates for various treatments. One might not give a damn about Irritable Bowel Syndrome, but reports of studies like one in the *American Journal of Gastroenterology* showing a 78% success rate with patients who were previously unresponsive to other treatment methods, or in *Lancet* where hypnosis showed a 95% rate for improvement of symptoms, one has to take notice! Again, these sections are heavily annotated with references to the research, so the numbers, especially when remarkable, certainly carry some weight.

Of course, there is quite a degree of variability here, with some cases (like the above) of hypnosis succeeding where other (medical) approaches didn't, to cases where hypnosis' effects were in *conjunction* with other therapies, and the numbers ranged from significant to extraordinary. As one might expect, much of what was most successful involved complaints with substantial "mind" components ... pain, stress, nervousness, etc. ... and less with "damage" issues, but even with problems such as lower back pain it's *"a tool that can be used as often as you need it, without side effects and without waiting."*

I, personally, would have appreciated more material on the *techniques* used in the various treatments, but that's no doubt due to my having practiced this a bit. If you have an interest in the clinical usage of hypnosis, or in medical treatments in general, you will likely find things to like about The Hypnosis Treatment Option[4]. It was, however, a whole lot more than I wanted/needed to know about these various conditions, and the *"and I can PROVE it!"* angle wore thin as well (however, I suppose that in medical publications having research citations for nearly every point may be *de rigueur* and expected). This definitely is one of those "your mileage may vary" situations, it's chock full of interesting info if you're into that particular thing, but probably "TMI" if you're not.

Notes:

1. http://btripp-books.livejournal.com/142252.html

2. http://www.librarything.com/wiki/index.php/HelpThing:Er_list

3-4. http://amzn.to/1iaYb0S

Tuesday, May 7, 2013[1]

"Don't be schtupid, be a schmarty ..."

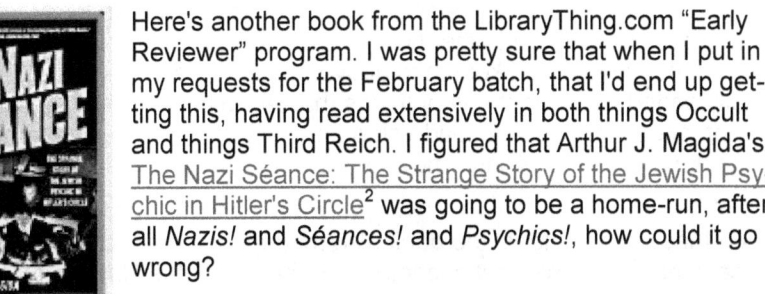

Here's another book from the LibraryThing.com "Early Reviewer" program. I was pretty sure that when I put in my requests for the February batch, that I'd end up getting this, having read extensively in both things Occult and things Third Reich. I figured that Arthur J. Magida's The Nazi Séance: The Strange Story of the Jewish Psychic in Hitler's Circle[2] was going to be a home-run, after all *Nazis!* and *Séances!* and *Psychics!*, how could it go wrong?

Unfortunately, Magida's book lacks all the drama and luridness that one might expect of its subject ... and veers fairly close to being something of a bait-and-switch. From the title/subtitle one might think that Erik Jan Hanussen was doing spiritualist parties for Hitler, and that the book was going to have a whole bunch of juicy details about these ... but the closest that it's *suggested* that Hanussen was in on-going touch with "Hitler's Circle" (note the omission of "Inner" in that) was that it appeared that he had knowledge about the notorious Reichstag fire in advance of its happening.

Is it the author's fault that the "fun read" that I'd anticipated the book being did not materialize? I'm sure that this sells better being marketed like a pulp novel than as a biography of a minor figure from Germany between the world wars ... but it's much more the latter than the former, and reading through it I kept waiting for it "to get good".

As a biography of Hanussen, it's quite good, and really remarkably well researched, given both the ephemeral nature of the psychic stage show, and the grinding obliteration of WW2 on the places he lived and worked. This is, on that level, a very interesting look into the work of psychic/spiritualist performance at the time, with many others aside from Hanussen discussed. Many of the details are impressive in that they were able to be retrieved (such as the deal that he got for a series of shows in Paris).

Hanussen himself is presented somewhat as an enigma, both a self-confessed "carny" playing his audiences, and a possible psychic, with a long string of otherwise-hard-to-explain revelations ... including the one that won him a major court case and ended up being a huge boost to his career. He also appears to have been a bit of a fool ... or certainly *deeply* naive ... in believing that Hitler and the Nazis were just "posturing" and would prove to be reasonable people. He was a strong supporter of the Fascist movement, publishing issue after issue of his magazine promoting Hitler as a savior of Germany, with glowing predictions for the future. Did he *believe* this, or figure he was being "useful" to the biggest, nastiest dog on the block? Needless to say, as a Jew, this seems to be an insane course to have taken, but somehow he dodged that reality for years.

In the book he has *one* significant Nazi contact, Count Wolfgang Heinrich von Helldorf, a high-ranking officer in Berlin, and a "fallen aristocrat" whose own estates had been frittered away. Hanussen provided Helldorf with the opportunity to enjoy the "rock star" wealth that he commanded on and off (along with some other "rock star" perks), and also ended up lending large sums to both Helldorf and other Nazi officers. Evidently Hanussen thought these connections would keep him above the dangers in the street, but they actually ended up being the very things that led to his murder. Certainly his other brushes with the Nazi leadership (such as a chilling encounter with Goebbels) makes one wonder how he was able to *not* see the danger of his situation.

Due to these connections, the book also manages to paint an picture of the "descent into madness" that accompanied the rise of the Nazi party. While not breaking any new ground on the subject, it provides a perspective not as well covered in other sources I've read (frankly, there are parts of The Nazi Séance[3] that resemble nothing quite so much as the tenser parts of *The Sound of Music!*).

Again, I was hoping for another look at the Occult underpinnings of the Nazi regime, as told from the perspective of the activities of Hanussen's career ... and there is very little of that in this book. As a biography of a performer who was delusional in regards to the evil he was sidling up to, it's a very well done study, but it's not what I (and I'm guessing most people would be) expecting. This has only been out a few months, so it should be available in your local brick & mortar book store (if you still have any near you), but it's rather telling that the new/used channel at the on-line big boys already have copies of this kicking around for under two bucks.

Notes:

1. http://btripp-books.livejournal.com/142397.html
2-3. http://amzn.to/1iaXAMC

Friday, May 17, 2013[1]

Me, I'm not a fanboy ...

This was one of those "business" books that I got from the good folks at McGraw Hill (I don't recall at this point if I asked for them to send me a review copy or if they queried me to see if I'd be interested in having a go at it), but it's obviously "in my wheelhouse". However, I again find myself in the minority on a business book, and wondering what others are seeing in a title that is escaping *me*. Ekaterina Walter's Think Like Zuck: The Five Business Secrets of Facebook's Improbably Brilliant CEO Mark Zuckerberg[2] has a very impressive 5-star rating over on Amazon, with 92 out of 103 giving it five stars, another 10 giving it four stars, and one lone reviewer giving it just one. While I'm not as negative about this as the 1-star reviewer was, I certainly agree with the thrust of his commentary.

Frankly, I'm surprised ... the author is, according to her jacket blurb:

> "a social innovator at Intel. A recognized business and marketing thought leader, she is a regular contributor to Mashable, Fast Company, Huffington Post, and other leading-edge print and online publications."

... etc., etc., etc. However, when she's writing about Zuckerberg she sounds *exactly* like my 13-year-old daughter extolling the virtues of Harry from (the current hot "boy band") One Direction! If the parts of the book where Walter is writing about Zuckerberg maintained the tone of the parts of the book where she's *not* writing about him, it would have been a far better work. This dichotomy could not be more pronounced here, and it was almost *embarrassing* reading it, as one gets the impression that when she's thinking of Zuckerberg she's only a hormone surge away from flinging undergarments at what I have to assume is a shrine to the guy in her home. Seriously.

That's the bad news. The good news is that the book is quite interesting when she's looking at everybody else. As is all too often the case, I'm again left to wonder where the editor was.

OK, so shall we cut to the chase? What, you might ask (were you paying attention to the subtitle above), *are* those "Five Business Secrets" of Mr. *billionaire* Mark Zuckerberg? The book takes its structure from them, with five chapters each covering one ... and all start with a "P":

> **Passion** – having passion to drive change.
>
> **Purpose** – having a vision and a higher purpose to execute your passion.
>
> **People** – building the team that will take your ideas and success to new heights.

Product – *creating innovative products.*

Partnerships – *building powerful partnerships with people who fuel imagination and energize execution.*

As regular readers of my reviews know, I'm a bit skittish about things that form an acronym, or are tortuously convoluted to fit a "cutesy" theme, so I had the start of that tic coming up when I looked at the Contents, but this is a rare case where the artificial structure at least does no egregious damage to the book.

While this does have aspects of being a long-form love-letter to Zuckerberg, it takes a look at a number of other companies (and their no-doubt somewhat less *dreamy* founders), including Threadless, CollegeHumor, TOMS, Dyson, and Zappos. Also of note here is the concept of the *intrapreneur*, a term she borrows from Edelman Digital's David Armano, which is defined as somebody who, in the example of Scott Monty, global head of social media for Ford, "helped fundamentally change the way the company engages with its customers online", or is somebody with a strong entrepreneurial streak who chooses to work within a large organization rather than creating their own (which, to me, sounds like a formula for a lot of on-going frustration, but I guess you'd have to pick your "large organization" carefully!).

I found the following the best summation of the "Passion" section:

> "I would actually go so far as to say that one doesn't have to be a genius to create something extraordinary. Sometimes average people are the ones who spearhead true change. And that is because they are willing to act on their passion. They are willing to be wrong, to risk everything. They are willing to fail, get up, and try again. Passion serves as a catalyst to the execution of an idea. Those who are passionate enough to pioneer true change are those most likely to deliver on it."

Again, the strength of the book is in the examples that Walter delves into other than Zuck, and there are many really instructive stories here which look at those companies. Here's something from the "People" chapter that sets up a story about Tony Hsieh and Zappos:

> "The <u>right</u> people are those people who share your beliefs, live your values and strive for the same purpose. Those are the people who will see the changes coming when you miss them and help you look in the right direction. Those are the people who will stay with you when times are tough and give their best in the worst of times."

To those familiar with Zappos, this is obviously leading up to the tale of how they developed their rather unique HR approach, which includes testing candidates for how *lucky* they feel they are, and offering new hires, a few months into their tenure at the company, to pay them a substantial bonus if they want to leave. Another interesting quote here is from CollegeHumor's Ricky Van Veen: *"I always hire people that are smarter than I am."*

Another idea that Walter injects into the "People" chapter is what she refers to as "The Hummingbird Effect of Leadership", noting that hummingbirds push the limits of what is generally thought of as possible, and their hearts take up 30 percent of their body mass. While this is something of a side-concept for the overall book, it's interesting to see what she holds to be the "10 qualities" of the Hummingbird effect: 1. Flexibility, 2. Management, 3. Agility, 4. Strategic Thinking, 5. Persistence, 6. Fearlessness, 7. Results-orientation, 8. Intuition, 9. Character, and 10. Personal Development.

Again, the best parts of this book is where the author is digging into the histories of *other* business leaders, like James Dyson not succeeding on the right configuration for a bagless vacuum until his *5,127th* attempt, or how William Hewlett and David Packard built HP through a common vision, in contrast to how many companies are driven by a Visionary/Builder team-up, with one expressing the dream, and the other the values of the company.

As noted, I believe that Think Like Zuck[3] would have been a *much* stronger book if somebody had stood next to the author with a bucket of cold water to dissuade her from the *"sqeeeeeeee ... ZUCKY!!!"* vibe that nearly every passage dealing with him has here. There certainly is interesting info about the genesis of Facebook in here, but it's so much harder to absorb than the insightful, analytical, material devoted to all those non-Zuckerberg examples. While I found the read useful for the good parts, it did have a "Tiger Beat" aftertaste, that was hard to shake. This has only been out since December, so you should have a decent shot at finding at the brick-and-mortar book vendors, but the on-line big boys have it presently at about ten bucks off of cover, which is probably your best bet if this sounds like something you want to venture into.

Notes:

1. http://btripp-books.livejournal.com/142800.html
2-3. http://amzn.to/1hUwuJ7

Saturday, May 18, 2013[1]

It's really what you pin ...

I believe that I reached out to the good folks at McGraw Hill to get a copy of this one ... I'd recently reviewed a similar book on the Pinterest platform and figured, hey ... the more the merrier. One of the challenges in putting out books about very new web entities is the speed at which they *change*, and one has to figure, if one is venturing into writing one, that it won't have a long useful life, unless you are able to convince your publisher to produce regular new versions. The book I reviewed last Fall came out within *weeks* of a major change to Pinterest (I believe it was the switch away to the "by invitation" model), so it was inaccurate to that extent from the get-go. While Jason Miles and Karen Lacey's Pinterest Power: Market Your Business, Sell Your Product, and Build Your Brand on the World's Hottest Social Network[2] has been out for while (about half a year), I'm looking at reviewing it within *weeks* (I'm guessing) of Pinterest implementing a new format across the entire user base (I'm not happy about that, frankly), so much of this is a "snapshot" of how the platform *was* at a given point in time.

Pinterest is a strange bird in the social media sphere ... it grew at a *big-bang*-like rate, with seemingly every scrapbooker with a computer jumping in to create virtual versions of her pasted-up visions of clothes, food, hairstyles, shoes, accessories, vacation spots, more shoes, more hairstyles, crafts, kids activities, etc., etc., .etc. ... with a gender mix that's about 85% female. However, unlike almost every other "social media platform", Pinterest appears to be able to *sell product*. One of the top "trainers" for Pinterest is Melanie Duncan[3], and she claims to have fallen into that role almost by accident when she discovered that her clothing business was getting most of its traffic and conversions from the pins she'd put up "just to be there". Oddly, the "pin" metaphor comes from its founder, Ben Silbermann's childhood hobby of collecting insects and *pinning* them onto boards ... a visual that I'm sure would be unpopular with most of the site's users!

Anyway, this is to preface the fact that I didn't particularly "connect" with Pinterest Power[4], as its focus is in the "clothing small business" niche ... no doubt a strong area for Pinterest demographically, but not something that's much on *my* radar. This is also a book where one author is the "expert" and the other is the "writer", with Jason Miles being the content person, having developed his wife's "Liberty Jane Clothing" company into a six-figure online business with strong social penetration, and Karen Lacey apparently the hired word-slinger. The foreword for this is by Susan Gregg Koger of ModCloth, and the model of their fashion focus carries through here, often quite specifically.

Pinterest, of course, is remarkable for its growth, going from nearly no users to being a monster in just two years:

> *"Four months from its launch, Pinterest had only 200 users ... For the first couple of years, Pinterest experienced the same steady growth rate – 40 to 50 percent or more per month. Those 200 users in the first quarter of 2010 quickly grew to over 11 million unique visitors in January 2011. In March 2012, Pinterest became the third largest social media website in the world and is still growing fast."*

While most of the thrust of the book is to the Esty/handcrafted market, there certainly are elements that are more targeted to a general business audience ... one example of this is the "Eight Keys to Becoming a Trusted Resource":

1. Pin your Passion.
2. The Devil's In The Details.
3. Impress, Inspire, Startle.
4. Let Yourself Shine.
5. Integrity.
6. Social Proof.
7. Guarantees and Testimonials.
8. Get Personal

One of the bad and good things in the book are the plethora of lists like these, as, while they break down the concepts into easily acted-on plans, there is no unifying structure to them. There are also sets of "Three P's" ... Principle, Practice, and Profit ... scattered through the book, which add commentary about the lists and/or material with which they're associated..

I have been a Pinterest user for a while now, but I'm certainly not a *typical* Pinterest user, and this may explain why I was constantly having "disconnects" with the information being doled out in the book. I end up pinning *something* several times a week, either things I've generated (these book reviews, interview videos, etc.) or stuff I've come across on Facebook, et al, that I think would fit on one of my "boards". I was very surprised to read here that *"approximately 80 percent of Pinterest images are actually re-pins"*, as I very rarely will outright re-pin somebody else's pin, and it's even a *rarer* occasion when somebody else re-pins something of mine onto *their* boards. From my experience, I would have guessed that number to be more in the 5% range!

Most of the massive success stories I've seen for Pinterest tend to cluster into two zones, small businesses in the style/fashion niche, and large corporations with products popular with the "mommy blogger" contingent. I was somewhat incredulous when I read the author report:

> *"In the first four months of our company's presence on Pinterest, we received just over 2,000 repins with referral links back to the website. We also re-*

> ceived over 7,000 actual visitors to our website from Pinterest. This means a 3:1 ratio of website visits per repin is reasonable and even conservative. For every repin, we can now estimate we'll receive at least three website visits."

Now, I've had Pinterest in the mix on a lot of projects, from literary to media to non-profit, etc., and the numbers that Miles reports here are at least *a hundred times* more robust than *anything* I've seen ... although, I must admit, the general thrust of what he's saying is in line with what Duncan said she saw for her fashion business.

This makes me think that Pinterest Power[5] is a book arising from a particular niche in the Pinterest landscape, and is operating within a "reality tunnel" specific to that niche, and that the material in the book, while having general applicability in terms of methodology, is likely to NOT be particularly predictive for success for any venture *outside* the realm in which Liberty Jane, ModCloth, DIY/Esty, and others operate. I seriously doubt that the rules of the universe of "darling suede pumps" would be applicable in one trending more to "efficient fuel pumps". The book *does* venture into other areas than clothing, however, dipping into discussions of non-profits, churches and colleges, but I doubt that these are seeing the same results as the folks selling "cute stuff".

While there are generally useful strategies, tricks, and tips here, it exists in a reality which is limited to, I believe, a certain market which is highly attractive to the particular Pinterest demographic, and I really wish the book was being more specifically presented with that in mind. Again, I'm not in that demographic, and have virtually no contact with that niche, so my main reaction through the book was *"in what universe?"*, but if you ARE in those distinctive orbits, this could very well be a great book for you to *"Market Your Business, Sell Your Product, and Build Your Brand"*.

Notes:

1. http://btripp-books.livejournal.com/143066.html
2. http://amzn.to/1iaUsQT
3. https://www.facebook.com/EntrepreneuressAcademy
4-5. http://amzn.to/1iaUsQT

Sunday, May 19, 2013[1]

The Fusion Fire Hose ...

A number of months ago I attended a BIGfrontier[2] talk featuring Lon Safko, who was out pitching his new book, The Fusion Marketing Bible: Fuse Traditional Media, Social Media, & Digital Media to Maximize Marketing[3] ... while I was familiar with his previous *The Social Media Bible*, it'd never attempted to plow through its massive 640 pages. Noting that this was of a much more manageable length, I reached out to the good folks at McGraw Hill to request a copy.

Safko is an interesting character, with a bio that reads like fiction, involving numerous companies, inventions, programs, etc., etc., etc. that he is credited with developing. The concept of "Fusion Marketing" (for which he apparently has patents pending) is relatively simple in its broad strokes, however, in being (as one would gather from the sub-title) an approach to using a mixture of traditional, digital, and social media in one's marketing efforts.

One of the key elements of this approach, though, is not so simple ... the "Safko Wheel!"[4] is a three-dimensional visualization tool that appears to be remarkably complicated (having not *bought* the book, I was never able to successfully get into the "free extras" parts of the book's site[5] - which requires a password that never seemed to materialize from other requests – and so didn't have an opportunity to play around with the kit), although, according to the book, that complexity enables one to chart optimal courses in one's marketing strategy.

Frankly, there is a lot of stuff in here (after all, he's discussing three forms of media, and the various individual aspects of each, *and* how to work them into a unified approach!), so it's a bit hard to give an over-view in more than the broadest strokes (as above), so I'm going to go the other way, and cherry-pick bits and pieces to give you a sense of what's in there.

In discussing "microblogging" (ie Twitter), he has an interesting guideline:

> Every tweet needs to have a WII-FM (What's In It For ME) or a IDKT (I Didn't Know That) value to your readers. If you can provide that you win. If you can't, hold the tweet.

... he follows that with a warning that he'll *unfollow* you if you tweet the mundane stuff about pets, food, and even complaining about transportation – which I can understand if that's *all* somebody tweets about, but, hey.

In another place he's discussing social networks, and rattles off more than a dozen names (a couple of which I hadn't heard of), and strongly recommended signing up for every one you come across. He then preemptively addresses the scoffing that would come with suggesting MySpace in the past few years, both by pointing out that (at the time of writing) it still had more members, 200 million, than Twitter and LinkedIn combined, and by noting:

> What percentage of 200 million random people would you consider to be potential customers? Would it be 1 percent? Or maybe ½ percent? Well, ½ of 1 percent of 200 million is 1 million potential customers. Even at 0.0005 percent, you'd still have 1,000 prospects. Choose any number you like and run the numbers again. What do you have to lose? There has never been another time in the history of marketing when you had the opportunity to reach 200 million people with your message.

Again, there is so much stuff here ... Safko is one of the few marketing voices that is still bullish on my old stomping grounds of Second Life, and that leads him into stories of opportunities his presence there generated. The book is full of examples of how company X did project Y and ended up with result Z ... each illustrating how these things work.

Which brings me back to the Safko Wheel ... this arose "by accident" initially when he was trying to explain to a visually-oriented client that there were 20 major tools outlined in his *Social Media Bible*, "not just Facebook and Twitter", which he illustrated by producing a 20-point starburst and placing the individual elements at each of the points. This worked for Social, and he had the idea to do similar patterns for "traditional" and digital media. The dynamic part of this system is making connections between these elements, an example he gives is putting *coupons* on the back of *business cards* as how this would generate new ideas.

He then shows a 40-point wheel of 20 traditional and 20 social elements, and notes that this provides 8.2×10^{47} possible connections, and that's squared to 8.2×10^{94} if you factor in *reverse* connections. Obviously, this is an insane number, but it suggests how this could spur new ways of approaching one's marketing. He does warn, however:

> ... if your marketing message is "Hey, I want you to come buy my stuff!" it doesn't matter how many different ways you communicate that message ... Tripling the number of times a customer gets an ineffective marketing message does not make that message any more persuasive. You cannot simply focus on the vehicles of communication if you are going to be successful with either traditional or social media.

Another thing that he's quite adamant that should be defined in one's marketing efforts is your business' "COCA" - Cost of Customer Acquisition – something that I'm guessing the MBAs out there are familiar with, but is likely a rather hazy concept for most small businesses. The examples he gives range from under ten bucks to several thousand dollars for high-ticket items like new homes ... and he points out that you can't accurately know your ROI unless you have a fix on your COCA, and spends several pages giving a plan of action of doing this sort of analysis with all your recent and upcoming campaigns.

In another section he talks about "Google Juice" and "Link Love" and comes up with some amazing numbers, including some that suggest that you really need to do a blog on WordPress because, for some reason, new posts on that platform are very strong within Google's ranking system. Of course, he also deals with videos, podcasts, email campaigns, even *door hangers* in the course of the book, so there is way, way too much to even get around to listing in a review. Additionally, for the smart-phone obsessed (hey, I *have* one, but I don't keep it on me 24/7) there are also over 100 QR codes pointing off to web resources all throughout the text.

Oh, and the "final" variation of the wheel? It's got three rings (yeah, like a circus), one on each axis (so it sort of is a sphere), each with 20 elements, for traditional, digital, and social media. I think "bazillions" of possible combinations is probably shorting that by magnitudes of magnitudes, but I'm sure not going to try to do the math.

All-in-all, The Fusion Marketing Bible[6] is a pretty amazing book, certainly in the "taking a drink from a firehose" type of experience. It is, however, a *marketing* book. It's not a philosophical look at various media types, it's not a "how can I make myself a better person" book, it's not a futurist's vision for tomorrow, this is about selling stuff and making money, and how to do that with maximum efficiency with the tools currently at hand. As such "your mileage may vary" for how awesome a read this will be for you. It came out last Fall, but it is a hot enough topic that I'm sure the brick-and-mortar guys are likely to have it on hand, but the on-line options are currently offering it at a fairly sizable discount. It's not for *everybody* but if you're in marketing, or the Social/Digital spheres, I'm pretty sure you'll like this one.

Notes:

1. http://btripp-books.livejournal.com/143267.html
2. http://bigfrontier.org/
3. http://amzn.to/1MMBA8O
4. http://www.thefusionmarketingbible.com/wp-content/uploads/2012/04/Red_Wheel_Step_4.jpg
5. http://www.thefusionmarketingbible.com/
6. http://amzn.to/1MMBA8O

Tuesday, May 21, 2013[1]

Dat's one speecy-spicy sundae!

As regular followers of these reviews will no doubt recall, I've read a good chunk of Seth Godin's books over the past several years, but there are still quite a number that I haven't gotten to as yet. Typically, when I read something that would make me think I'd like to check out a book, and am not in a position to "pull the trigger" on getting it (either due to not wanting it badly enough to pay discount-from-retail, or not badly enough that I don't need it on this end of my vast stacks of "to be read" books, both physical and potential), I'll drop it onto my Amazon wish list where I can surf through and see if anything has dipped into the "cheap enough" zone with the new/used vendors to move me to ordering. Well, towards the end of last year, Godin's Meatball Sundae: Is Your Marketing Out of Sync?[2] hit whatever magic price point was in my head (that with $3.99 shipping seemed reasonable), and I got a copy.

Now, I need to indulge in a bit of a *mea culpa* here … I finished reading this *five months* ago, so it's really not very fresh up in my grey matter, and (unlike a lot of other books) it managed to run past my eyeballs without getting a forest of little bookmarks stuck in it to lead me back to choice passages/concepts, so I'm pretty much having to wing it in terms of being pithy in my commentary. I really do try to crank out these reviews within a couple of weeks of reading a book, but I hit a long stretch there when I just *could not* get a review out. It was just these past few weeks when "the dam broke" and I've been back to sitting in Starbucks all night punching away on my little netbook[3]. So, my apologies up front if this doesn't end up being the most *fluid* review I've done of one of Godin's books.

One other thing I suppose I should note, Meatball Sundae[4] came out in 2007, which is six years ago, which is, of course, *forever* in social media and/or digital marketing time. To give you an idea of what that means, the 3rd largest Social Media platform today, Pinterest, wouldn't even be founded for 3 years, Facebook was only a year past requiring that members have an .edu address and still had less than 100 million users, and MySpace was the big dog on the social block. I've noted this sort of "platform disconnect" previously (and, as I recall, in regards to some of Godin's earlier works), but what keeps these books attractive is that they're more ventures into the *philosophy* of marketing, within the context of new tools and realities, and less *manuals* on how to use any particular tool out there.

What I'm going to do in this review is to pretty much just "cherry-pick" bits and pieces that sound good to me, and try to weave them together into something that will at least give you a sense about what the book's about. To start out, here's where Godin defines the freaky title:

> *A meatball sundae: messy, disgusting, ineffective. The result of combining two perfectly good items that don't go well together.*
>
> *The meatballs are the basic staples, the things that people need, the stuff that used to be marketed quite effectively with TV ads and other mass-market techniques.*
>
> *The topping is the New Marketing. MySpace, Web sites, YouTube, permission marketing, and viral techniques are all part of the magic that makes up the top of the sundae.*

Godin warns of the "shiny new thing" (and aggressive consultants pushing it) obsession … and furthers the analogy here:

> *People treat New Marketing like a kid with a twenty-dollar bill at an ice cream parlor. They keep wanting to add more stuff – more candy bits, and sprinkles and cream and cherries. The dream is simple: "If we can just add enough of [today's hot topping], everything else will take care of itself."*

Now, considering what I noted a few paragraphs up from here, one would think the *last* thing that I'd point out would be the author's prognostication of *trends*, but it really *is* Godin's genius to sense how things are moving and in which direction, and while some of these may have played out in quite different particulars than what he was envisioning in the ancient days of 2007, the 14 trends he lays out that are "completely remaking what it means to be a marketer" still sound solid today:

> *Trend 1: Direct communications and commerce between producers and consumers.*
>
> *Trend 2: Amplification of the voice of the consumer and independent authorities.*
>
> *Trend 3: Need for an authentic story as the number of sources increases.*
>
> *Trend 4: Extremely short attention spans due to clutter.*
>
> *Trend 5: The long tail.*
>
> *Trend 6: Outsourcing.*
>
> *Trend 7: Google and the dicing of everything.*
>
> *Trend 8: Infinite channels of communications.*
>
> *Trend 9: Direct communication and commerce between consumers and consumers.*
>
> *Trend 10: The shifts in scarcity and abundance.*
>
> *Trend 11: The triumph of big ideas.*
>
> *Trend 12: The shift from "how many" to "who".*
>
> *Trend 13: The wealthy are like us.*
>
> *Trend 14: New gatekeepers, no gatekeepers.*

Personally, I felt that Meatball Sundae[5] was worth the price of admission for the story of "The Man Who Invented Marketing" ... which you probably would take a very, very long time to hit with unaided guesses, as he dates back to the mid-1700s! This was Josiah Wedgewood, who went from being a potter's apprentice in a little village to being the head of a *brand* which still thrives centuries later. Godin equates the cultural changes of Wedgewood's time (which he was able to exploit by approaching his family's trade in a radical new manner) with those of our current era, and this is a story (really, it's worth the cost of the book – especially via the used vendors, a "like new" copy of the hardcover will only set you back six bucks with shipping right now!) is something that will resonate in all the right channels, and be a touchstone for moving forward in new modes.

Speaking of new modes, Godin says we're operating in the *fourth* industrial revolution, the first coming in the late 1700s with the introduction of factory work with Wedgewood being an exemplar of that era, the second coming in the late 1800s through the 1950s with Henry Ford typifying that style of business, this was followed by the third which was fed by mass marketing and the post-war booms, with information, coordination and communication being the key components, GE's Jack Welch is the figure Godin identifies with this. The fourth is driven by the web and "new marketing", and this is creating changes, new industries rising from the ashes of niches devastated by the Internet's dynamics.

I'm going to close with two randomly picked pieces (well, they *were* on the pages that had bits of paper stuck in), the first is that "interruption=SPAM" ... where in the 3rd revolution, you could load up the TV schedule with interruptions – commercials – and deliver your message, in the new model, any interruptions are resented as much as "unsolicited commercial email". Secondly (and to some extant, "cutting to the chase"):

> *If you want to thrive, you need to do two things:*
> Make something worth talking about;
> and make it easy to talk about.

As noted above, this has been around a while, so might not be in your local surviving brick-and-mortar book vendor, but the on-line big guys have it, and at a *remarkable* discount (currently *71% off*, making it about a wash with the "like new" used copies, when their individual shipping charges have been added!). Despite it being a bit "antique" in the particulars, I really enjoyed reading it,and if you've got an interest in marketing, and the current trends in communication, you are likely to get a good deal out of this (above and beyond the Wedgewood story).

Notes:

1. http://btripp-books.livejournal.com/143531.html
2. http://amzn.to/1hUsAjg
3. http://statigr.am/p/460300917002183472_8963303
4-5. http://amzn.to/1hUsAjg

Tuesday, May 21, 2013[1]

A little review of a very bad time ...

This was one of those dollar store finds ... picked up as much for its brevity (this is definitely a one-afternoon read) as for its topic. Starting Over: Why the Last Decade Was so Damn Rotten and Why the Next One Will Surely Be Better[2] by *Fortune Magazine's* managing editor Andy Serwer is, as one would guess, a review of the "00's" and all the crappy stuff that happened over those years. The first half of the book is primarily taken up by a year-by-year rundown of the "top stories" from 2000 to 2009 ... a decade that has been called "the Decade From Hell" and

> "... began with 9/11, ended with the financial meltdown, and had Katrina in the middle. They also had Saddam Hussein, the invasion of Afghanistan, Abu Ghraib, the tsunami in Southeast Asia, and Bernie Madoff. Sorry to depress you."

This part of the book is pretty "thin on content", with an iconic (bad news) photo on one page being paired with a run-down (in 50-60 words or so) of notable (bad news) story headers. These, and the introduction take up 45% of the book, with the remnant being essays on various thematic trends in the decade's news. These are: "In The Beginning" (opening with a pic of one of the jetliners about to plow into the World Trade Center), "The Great Meltdown", "What Went Wrong", "Not Just Acts of God", "Starting Over", and "The Promise".

Of course, this all started around midnight on December 31, 1999 when the whole world was holding its breath (and hoarding food, water, and fuel!), expecting the Y2K bug to bring civilization to its knees,

> "Instead, it was the American Dream that was about to dim. Bookended by 9/11 at the start and a financial wipe-out at the end, the first 10 years of this century will very likely go down as the most dispiriting and disillusioning decade that Americans have lived through in the post-World War II era."

Sometimes Serwer does posit answers ... in the "What Went Wrong" chapter he lists Neglect (warning signs of Islamicism), Greed (the go-go mortgage years), Self-Interest (labor unions gutted major industries, unwilling to admit to a changing manufacturing landscape), and Deferral of Responsibility (infrastructure decay, contributing to the Katrina destruction). He also cites the undoing of the regulatory Glass-Steagal act in 1999 which then allowed for disastrous mixing of banking functions, and re-writing of rules that allowed firms like Bear Stearns and Lehman to *"pile $30 of debt onto each $1 of capital"*.

In the "Starting Over" chapter he revisits the same things looked at in "What Went Wrong", and suggests ways that we're going to address these things in new ways, and then takes a deeper look forward in "The Promise":

> "I tend to think of technologies as waves," says Peter Bishop of the University of Houston. "My candidate for the next wave is biotechnology." Bishop believes that "we will finally get our arms around how to manipulate code for DNA, create synthetic organisms as a platform, and then design how we want those things to work for food, for energy, and of course then extending it into human health."
>
> And the holy grail of this century, finding and optimizing energy sources beyond oil, gas, and coal, will naturally entail technological expertise – think batteries, as well as solar, wind, and geothermal – and likely even biotechnologial prowess. Bishop gives an example: "Biofuels, particularly algae, are probably going to really boom. I think we're going to see large algae farms, where you need three resources – water, sunlight, and a source of carbon dioxide, because grabbing it out of the air isn't efficient enough. So you'll put an algae farm next to a coal plant or a natural gas plant and try to pump CO_2 into the algae and then turn the algae into a biofuel."

Again, this is a *slim* volume, well under 100 pages all told, and how you like it possibly is a function of what price you find it for ... the buck it cost me at the dollar store was not misspent, but if you shelled out the $14.95 cover price you might feel somewhat gypped (as many reviewers of it have). The on-line big boys do have it at a substantial discount (nearly 2/3rds off), which makes it cheaper (as an add-on for an order that will have free shipping) than getting a copy from the new/used vendors, whose lowest priced copies (at this moment) are all hanging just under two bucks ... odd for a book that's been dumped into the dollar store channel. Starting Over[3] is an interesting enough read, if somewhat of a major bummer, and largely stands as a reminder of what we've survived on our way into the current maelstrom dragging down into insolvency, tyranny, and societal madness ... heck, the way things are going, in another decade those double-zero years might be seen as "the good old days"!

Notes:

1. http://btripp-books.livejournal.com/143854.html

2-3. http://amzn.to/1JS6yr9

Saturday, May 25, 2013[1]

Well, here's another nice Mesh ...

Although I'm sure my wife will argue otherwise, I am able to consider suggestions, especially when the subject is books. Heck, I'll read stuff just because I was able to get it for a buck at the dollar store. So, when the manager of the Capital One 360 Chicago Café[2] (which provides my client Nature's Little Recylcers'[3] name-sake worms with a generous diet of used espresso grounds) asked if I'd read Lisa Gansky's The Mesh: Why the Future of Business Is Sharing[4], I had to say "no", and admit to not having heard of it previously. She was highly recommending it, so I went right to the computer when I got home and found a used copy off the web.

The concept of "The Mesh" is very easy for *me* to wrap my head around, living downtown and without a car, I end up using, with some frequency, one of the shining examples of a "mesh business", ZipCar. If you're from "the land beyond public transit", ZipCar is a service that rents cars by the hour, and has hundreds of them scattered around the downtown in various garages and parking lots. You connect either on the computer or via your phone, pick a car you want to reserve, and block out the hours you need (assuming they're available – most weekends around here the two in our building book fast) ... you have a membership card with an NFC chip that, when placed over a reader inside the windshield, will unlock the car if it's reserved to you then – the keys are in it. What's awesome on this service is that the insurance and gas are included for about a total of $12-15/hr.

Car sharing is a perfect example of a business that's in the "sweet spot" for a mesh business. There's a graphic in the book which is very useful, a 2x2 grid with "frequency of use" on the X axis and "cost" on the Y axis. Low-cost, frequently used items (the illustration shows toothpaste and a brush) are not particularly good for a mesh business as there's no reason not to personally own them, low cost, seldom used items (here, a hammer) are also not ideal as the cost of rental is likely to be relatively close to the cost of owning, and high cost, frequently used items (a smartphone is pictured) aren't good, because the "sharing" aspect is not well supported. It's things up in the top right quadrant of infrequently used expensive items that Gansky identifies as the "mesh sweet spot".

Of course, this concept is not new, normal car rental, or even arguably public transit, fit the general outlines, and hardware stores have been renting carpet cleaning equipment for decades ... the difference being that current technology makes it possible to fine-tune the process. She identifies two variations, the "Full Mesh" like ZipCar *"... meaning that the company owns and maintains the vehicles. By participating, I get the benefits associated with owning, but without the hassles and cost."* The other is the "Own-to-Mesh" model where *"they create a platform for people who own things to share them easily and profitably.*", with examples of companies that allow folks to rent out their homes while they travel.

> Both the Full Mesh and Own-to-Mesh models are most successful when the customer feels empowered by relinquishing or sharing ownership. Mesh businesses are well positioned to constantly improve their customers' convenience by refining the overall experience, while offering them long-term savings and near-term happy surprises. Those ingredients will make sharing irresistible – customers will choose access to superior goods and services over living with lots of stuff.

The Mesh[5] features a lot of stories of businesses that have either Mesh or mesh-like business models ... such as Blockbuster's Wayne Huizenga, who had previously been into waste management, renting dumpsters in New York City ... she quotes him as saying *"I'm all about renting – I buy it once, and wherever it moves, I keep making money on my old investment."* ... obviously he was able to take that sensibility into the video tape market, although didn't have a way to save that being almost totally swept away by digital, web-delivered, video. This is why Netflix has emerged as such a strong player, while the "traditional" video businesses faded away. One of the thing missing in the older rental models was interaction with the customer base ... she talks of a "virtuous cycle of trust": Learn – Trust – Play – Engage ... where you build trust, grow your base, and refine the offers based on feedback from the customers. Again, this is something made far easier to accomplish with the rise of the web and mobile technologies.

She introduces another 4-cell chart which addresses this, with the X axis being frequency of sharing (toasters vs. taxis, for instance), and the Y axis being "data enabled goodness" (socks vs. a GPS device), and only in the high frequency sharing and high date-enabled quadrant are there successful "mesh businesses" (here listing four: iTunes, Netflix, ZipCar, and Amazon Web Services).

Perhaps the weakest part of the book here is that it is largely *theoretical*, talking about numerous situations, conditions, opportunities, market forces, demographic shifts, and various other trends (she even manages to wedge in global warming) ...but there are few entities as clearly "meshy" as ZipCar, so a lot of what is discussed are companies that have projects or divisions which are heading in a Mesh direction or have Mesh-like elements.

It's not that she didn't *try*, as the last quarter of the book is "The Mesh Directory", an abbreviated version of an on-line resource ("Mesh – The Pulse of the Sharing Economy" at http://meshing.it/[6]) which lists hundreds of companies over 27 categories that Gansky has decided are "meshy" enough (although, some, like Klout, LinkedIn, or MeetUp seem to be more there for the name-check than being particularly mesh-like in my understanding of the concept).

This was certainly an interesting book, and I have a bunch of bookmarks in it that will lead me off to subsequent researches. As I've been noting of late ... it *is* a "business book" so is likely not a lot of readers' cup of tea, but if you are trying to keep up with trends in the culture, this is a good window into something that's likely to be growing in influence. The Mesh[7] *has* been out for a while (fall of 2010), so it might be spotty in the physical book stores, but the big boys have it on-line, and you can snag a new copy of the paperback for 1¢ and the hardback for under two bucks through the new/used vendors (plus, of course, the $3.99 shipping).

Notes:

1. http://btripp-books.livejournal.com/143925.html
2. https://www.facebook.com/CapitalOne360Chicago
3. http://natureslittlerecyclers.com/
4-5. http://amzn.to/1hUqBvp
6. http://meshing.it/
7. http://amzn.to/1hUqBvp

Sunday, May 26, 2013[1]

When is a dummy not a dummy?

Now, *this* one's going to be a bit hard to review, because, well ... it's a "quick reference" work! As those of you who may have been *stalking* me over the years of my putting up these reviews will likely know, I've been not only *on* the web since the very early days (I bought my first computer in 1982, and was on-line with Plink, Genie, CI$, Prodigy, etc. soon after), but I've been writing web sites since as early as 1995 (when there were nearly no resources, aside from university computer departments, for learning how to code). I went back to school in 2002-2003 and took a diploma in "Web Development & Business Programming", in which I was *very* good (got a 4.0 in a curriculum that 95% of the incoming students "washed out of"), but that didn't help when it came to finding a job in the post-"dot-com bubble burst" economy where there were dozens of programmers with years of experience in line in front of me for every available job. I recently became aware that much of my coding was relying on decade (or longer) old standards, and had heard all sorts of "bells and whistles" that were becoming available in HTML5 and CSS3 ... so signed up for a course in these a few months back.

This is to preface why I ended up in possession of a copy of Andy Harris' HTML5 For Dummies Quick Reference[2]. Over the years, I've found the "For Dummies" books a good place to start on something that I either didn't know about, or needed a refresher on. They are a mixed bag, however, with some being excellent, and some being notably awful. This, while being a "quick reference" (there are numerous code examples throughout the book and executed on the author's web site), and not intended to be a "course", was quite informative and encompassing of the subject – if being a bit of a mass of info to try to take in all at once as a "read". Oh, and just in case there are total code newbs reading this, HTML is Hyper Text Markup Language, and CSS is Cascading Style Sheets ... I know my wife would be hard pressed to break those out, so I figure the might be a few who were similarly unfamiliar with the abbreviations that had still read this far down!

One thing that really surprised me in getting into HTML5 is that we're back to browser-specific code. "Back in the day" one pretty much had to write *two* web sites, one for Netscape, one for MSIE, and set up a "sniffer" on your index page that would send the right browser to the right code. For the past decade, this hasn't been so much of a problem ... well, here we are again when it comes to HTML5. There are lots of the new fancy stuff that will require "stacking" up code to specify the functions for the various browser engines, of which there are four main ones: WebKit – Chrome/Safari, Gecko – FireFox/Mozilla, Trident – MSIE, and Presto – Opera. Between these there is a *maddening* mix of implementations, as one can see by the charts on this page[3] (that Harris points his readers to).

Anyway, that being noted, let's look at the book. The first couple of chapters put HTML5 in context of the development of mark-up languages, and go over the HTML basics. It then looks at "New or Changed HTML5 Elements", including Semantic Page Elements, Inline Semantic Elements, Media Elements, and Ruby Elements. Next is "New and Modified Form Elements" broken down into New Form Elements, New Form Element Attributes, and New Form Input Types. While these might not sound particularly exciting, there are all sorts of handy new things in there. The book then moves to an overview of using CSS and some of the basics (useful to me, since most of my coding has been pre-CSS!), before moving to "New and Improved CSS Elements" with CSS3's New Selection Tools, Downloadable Fonts *{finally!}* and Text Support, Flexible Box Layout Model *{"I will try to not write tables, I will try to not write tables, I will try to not write tables ..."}*, and New Visual Elements *{Gradients! Rounded Corners! Shadows! Reflections! Transparency! Whooo....}*. The penultimate chapter, "Changes in JavaScript" is a bit technical, but updates on some of the new things available for interfacing web sites with servers, etc. - a lot of this was a bit "over my head", frankly. Finally, there is "Working with the Canvas" ... the new "canvas" element being sufficiently flexible that the author's opted to pull it out for its own chapter, and a look at how other elements and tools (and CSS and JavaScript) work in relation to it. You can visit his page[4] with the code samples to see some of these in action.

Again, you're probably not going to *learn* the ins-and-outs of writing HTML5 from this reference, but if you're messing with it and think *"oh, heck, how did that shadow thing work?"*, you're a quick flip to the Index away from finding out the specifics with this. One of the things I'm most excited about here is the ability to write in fonts that are not dependent on what the end-user has installed on their system ... a *huge* leap forward for web design.

HTML5 for Dummies[5] is probably going to be available "wherever programming books are sold", but the online new/used vendors have "new" copies for under three bucks (plus shipping, of course), which might be a good thing to think about if you are, like I was, living in an earlier realm of code. It goes without saying, however, that this isn't for *everybody*, or even for most of the folks reading these reviews ... but I'd recommend it to anybody who's not a massive code wiz, who wants to keep up with what's out there these days!

Notes:

1. http://btripp-books.livejournal.com/144382.html
2. http://amzn.to/1JsoeHI
3. https://en.wikipedia.org/wiki/Comparison_of_layout_engines_%28HTML5%29
4. http://aharrisbooks.net/h5qr/
5. http://amzn.to/1JsoeHI

Wednesday, June 5, 2013[1]

On instituting something new ...

I heard Jeffrey Phillips speak at a Big Frontier[2] event last fall, after which I contacted the good folks at McGraw Hill to get a review copy of his Relentless Innovation: What Works, What Doesn't – And What That Means For Your Business[3] . Unfortunately, I got done reading this just when I "hit the wall" on my reviewing, and wasn't able to get caught up with it for several months (and when I *did* get back into writing, this had meandered off into the hands of an associate, and I only just got it back this past weekend!). For those familiar with these rambling riffs off of regulation reviewing will recognize, I'm going into that near-TMI detail to cop a plea to this not being particularly fresh in my head … and I am hoping to have your forgiveness for not producing the most razor-sharp analysis here today!

Frankly, when I got into the book, I was expecting something more of a rabble-rousing manifesto-like tome, as his *presentation* on it was quite energetic and focused on companies that were "relentlessly" innovating, and comparing these to those who were *not*. However, the book itself is much more muted and level-headed, going into a lot of analysis about what causes various businesses to manifest innovation styles all along that spectrum. So, my *first impression* was that I kept "waiting for it to get good", and never quite finding the visceral "rah-rah" rollercoaster that I must have been hoping for. Of course, that's *me*, and the disappointment I felt was hardly the fault of Phillips or his book!

I don't usually do this, but I'm dipping into Phillips' web page for some context … who is this guy, and what does he really know about innovation? Well, he's a principal at OVO, a consultancy specializing in innovation. Here's a bit of their defining what they're about:

> Every business started out as an idea. As companies grow, innovation skills rapidly become dormant. Like a limb that atrophies from lack of use, innovation skills require more engagement and constant exercise. We believe innovation must become a consistent business discipline, rather than an occasional or sporadic event initiated in response to a competitive threat.

Essentially, Relentless Innovation[4] is a long-form expansion on that statement, textured by bringing in an anti-innovation arch-villain: "BAU"- Business As Usual (*"innovation threatens BAU more than almost any other initiative"*). The bastions of BAU are those in Middle Management – the c-suite may be behind an innovation, and the foot soldiers will follow whatever orders come down, but *"... middle managers know they'll bear the burden of* any suggested change to the model and they will have to clean up any mistakes ... they are the employees most likely to rush to {the BAU's} defense."

Phillips goes into how MBA-favorite systems, like Six Sigma and Lean, lock many businesses into models in which innovation is nearly impossible: *"The business of big business is efficiency and predictability, not innovation ... we have refined the operating model to the extent that innovation has become a threat to how firms operate, rather than a potential benefit."* Again, while CEOs constantly list "innovation" as one of their top 3 priorities, less than 25% of manufacturing firms and less than **8%** of service firms had created new products or services within the preceding three years!

After decades of applying "shop-floor" efficiency improvement models across the entire enterprise, most businesses are ill-equipped to indulge in innovation, with executives whose expertise is down-sizing and streamlining:

> *In an era when predictability is the hallmark of an excellent executive ... innovation's upredictability leaves executives exposed ... since the compensation of many executives is tied to their stock price ... surprises, <u>even positive ones</u> ... aren't usually welcome.*

The author identifies eight factors that "create an innovation BAU framework" within organizations that have been successful in their dedication to innovation:

1. innovation metrics tied to specific goals
2. compensation
3. enabling functions
4. who we manage versus what we manage
5. communication
6. defined processes
7. reactive versus proactive philosophy
8. human resources and talent management

He details examples such as Proctor & Gamble, who had a goal that 50% of ideas would originate from *outside* the company, despite its substantial internal R&D resources ... in 2009 they had five of the top ten new product launches in the U.S., so that would appear to be paying off. Another example is that of 3M, whose goal was that *"30 percent of the revenue generated in any year should come from products that are less than four years old"* ... causing them to "not sit on their laurels" of established moneymakers. He quotes the "VP of Innovation" at RJ Reynolds on their model of "setting fences", things which they seek to achieve, then have the next goal already defined. Google is shown as an example of how compensation is revised to encourage follow-through on innovation which might otherwise have been threatening to the checks of those responsible for steering these projects – they get a stake in the on-going success of the products developed. Sometimes companies need to separate out the innovation, like IBM which developed an Emerging Business Organization in response to its previous failures to get new projects past their deeply-entrenched BAU cultures.

How does a corporation institute innovation in its ranks? *"Few firms succeed using ad hoc or "on the fly" innovation processes".* ... but Phillips details what does generally work:

> A well-defined innovation process will encompass an entire "end to end" innovation capability, including these phases:
>
> - Trend spotting and scenario planning.
> - Gathering customer needs and market insights.
> - Generating ideas using the scenarios and needs as guideposts.
> - Evaluating, prioritizing, and selecting ideas for further development.
> - Prototyping and piloting ideas.
> - Transitioning ideas into product or service development.
> - Launching new products and services.

One counter-example given is the legendary Xerox PARC operation, which seeded much of what has become the personal computer revolution, but they *"struggled to move new ideas out of the research lab and into product development."* and innovation after innovation ended up being the core of *other* companies' products.

Much of the book reads like a report from a consultant to a company, with a lot of "what you should do", which makes it a bit less appealing to the "general reader" as most are not in a position to actually implement any of this. While I would have preferred to have Relentless Innovation[5] shifted over into a more "philosophical" look at innovation, that would no doubt be less *useful* to the author and his firm when using it as an introduction to their services!

This has only been out for six months or so, and is likely to still be readily available through your local book vendor which handles business titles ... however, the on-line big boys have it at about $1/3^{rd}$ off of cover price, and the new/used guys (oddly) have "new" copies for around ¼ of cover (plus shipping, of course). Perhaps if I was in an upper executive position in a large company, this would have been a more gripping read, but while it was full of interesting stuff, it was evidently "not written for me", and I suspect that the further the reader is from the corner offices, the less connection they'll have with this ... so consider that as a caveat to my general liking of the book.

Notes:

1. http://btripp-books.livejournal.com/144548.html

2. http://www.bigfrontier.org/index.php?option=com_content&view=section&layout=blog&id=4&Itemid=10

3-5. http://amzn.to/1S4oVjt

Monday, June 10, 2013[1]

Step right up ...

This one came to me through a somewhat convoluted route. The author (and noted speaker/trainer) Brendon Burchard was wanting to help his friend Paulo Coelho's new book *Manuscript Found in Accra* get a big boost over on Amazon, and he offered, were one to *buy* Coelho's book, and send Burchard the receipt, to send out a copy of this book, *and* give access to one of his on-line courses. So, Life's Golden Ticket[2] showed up in my mailbox.

I'd previously reviewed Burchard's The Millionaire Messenger[3], which is pretty much a training manual for folks interested in getting into the "information marketing" business. In that, however, he repeatedly referred back to Life's Golden Ticket[4], which he wrote following a near-fatal car crash that had re-set what he saw for the rest of his life. From his descriptions in that book, I had anticipated that this was going to be a deep, philosophical, look at the nature of being, and how one might make better choices, etc. ... after all, this is the book that he based his entire speaking/selling career on ... and I was somewhat expecting a minor-league version of *In Search of the Miraculous* or similar examination of the human condition. This book is not that ... not by a long shot ... but I do get the sense that on some level the author would like it to be held in those circles.

There is a sub-title to the paperback copy that Burchard sent ... "An Inspirational Novel" ... and that is, perhaps, telling. This does seek to be inspirational ... that's clear all the way through, but it has more the narrative flow of "allegory" books (*Flatland*, is an example that comes to mind) than a novel per se. There's not much of a "story arc" here, not much character development (aside from the protagonist's, and that's limited), just a run through set pieces constructed to bring out some point about personality and worldview.

Now, as those of you who regularly read my reviews will realize, I "don't do novels" (much like my drinking, I consumed what I was going to of fiction back in my teens and 20s), so I don't have the "tap-dancing" skills needed to safely discuss this without giving out "spoilers" ... something that I'm aware (from the constant wailing about that expressed over on the boards discussing reviews on LibraryThing.com!) is a major issue for some. Frankly, the thought occurred to me that *any* discussion of this would "spoil" it for a certain type ... so, if you suspect that you're *one of those*, just quit reading now. Take it that I liked it well enough, and skip down to the last paragraph if you're interested in the availability/ordering stuff that I usually close with.

{Insert Jeopardy theme[5] here while we wait.}

OK, have the spoilerphobes left us? River Song? Alrighty, then ...

First of all, the stuff about his actual car crash just take up about 3 pages in an introduction. I was really expecting this to be more concrete and reality-based. Nope. The book starts off with the protagonist hearing a news report about his fiancée, who had disappeared 40 days previously (leaving him as a prime suspect of the police), followed quickly by a call from her mother. She, Mary, has been found on a highway nearly dead ... and he rushes to the hospital. She looks to be dying, and he wants to stay with her, but she *insists* that he take an envelope out of her coat and take it to an old abandoned amusement park, and give it to her brother. Needless to say, he thinks she's delusional, but this sounds very much like a "last wish" and she's quite insistent that he go there right away.

Oh, delusional ... her brother had *died* at that amusement park 20 years previously, and that was one of the reasons it was no longer in business. So, he takes the blood-spattered envelope and drives off (much to the chagrin of her parents). When he reaches the park, he finds her car still in the parking area. As he approaches the park, things start to shift, and rather than the empty ruin of a park, there are people, rides, vendors, etc., all there. He, however, does not have a ticket to get in, and this presents a problem, until he is "vouched for" by an elderly custodian, Henry.

Now, one of the reasons I quit reading fiction was that I found myself constantly getting irritated with poorly defined characters, holes in the plot, etc., and I kept waiting for Henry to get "filled out" more. By the end of the story, there is a *bit* more detail on him, but still not enough for him to be anything other than a psychopomp ... and here a literary contrivance to get the protagonist from locale to locale. There is no explanation *why* he takes the protagonist under his wing, and enabling (evidently rather extraordinarily) the protagonist to enter the park. I kept guessing scenarios, but that never gets outlined.

The protagonist is taken on a tour of the various rides and tents and features of the amusement park, some plausible, some purely fantastic, and introduced (or put into the hands of) various characters there. Many of these are clearly hostile to his presence in the park, and dismayed that Henry has taken the action to allow him to be there. In each scenario, he's "taught a lesson" about his life, be it battling with his father on a pirate ship, dealing with "other selves" in a hall of mirrors, being featured in a high-wire act, or being forced to deal with lions in a cage (while the location is described as an amusement park, much of what's there seems from a circus). Some stops are more successful than others, and in each case he gets passed back to Henry to continue the tour.

OK ... big spoiler coming up ... turn away now if you want to avoid it! It turns out that the various characters at the park only have a particular life span there, and by allowing the protagonist in, Henry used up the last of whatever it was that was keeping him there. As the book goes on he gets weaker, frailer, and sicker, and eventually "walks off stage" in the main tent. What linearity there had been in the story pretty much wanders off at that point, as Burchard is evidently attempting to tie the last loose ends together in the final chapter or two. When the protagonist is finally made to leave the park (he had "three strikes" on a particular set of rules), Mary and her parents are waiting for him in the parking area … some 40 days after he left her at the hospital to go there.

Again, Life's Golden Ticket[6] is not my usual sort of a read. I quite enjoyed it for the first half, was somewhat irritated by the second half, and felt it was an interesting "allegorical tale" that had to, regrettably, be forgiven its implausibilities (despite how much I would have preferred it to be more straight-forward). As noted above, I was totally expecting this to be a completely different sort of a book, but I know that there are those out there who like this type of thing quite a lot, and if you're one of them, it will probably be quite useful to you.

I don't know how readily available this would be in the brick-and-mortar book channels … it's certainly still in print, so would be obtainable there, if it's not on the shelves … but the on-line big boys have the paperback at a moderate discount, and the new/used guys are offering new copies for as little as a buck and a half … plus you could get this (and his other titles) directly from the author at http://www.brendonburchard.com/[7] (and sign up for his training courses if you're so inclined). This is another case of my wishing the book was something that it was not, yet finding it a decent enough read, with useful enough info … and I'm a cranky, non-fiction reading cynic, so you're likely to enjoy this far more than I managed to!

Notes:

1. http://btripp-books.livejournal.com/144832.html
2. http://amzn.to/1VHi3rA
3. http://btripp-books.livejournal.com/138306.html
4. http://amzn.to/1VHi3rA
5. http://www.televisiontunes.com/Jeopardy_-_2008_-_Think_Music.html
6. http://amzn.to/1VHi3rA
7. http://www.brendonburchard.com/

Friday, July 19, 2013[1]

A how-to for growing a business ...

This was a fairly unusual book to crop up on LibraryThing.com's "Early Reviewer" list ... which tends to be rather thin on non-fiction most months, and very rarely has "business" books. The LTER "almighty algorithm" (which matches books against requesting members' libraries) obviously saw the slew of business books I've been through over the past several years and figured that this needed to come to me. Frankly, being involved in a bare-bones bootstrapping start-up at the moment (but one with a very aggressive expansion plan), having a book that was geared to growing a business was of particular interest (although not specifically in my area!), and so I jumped right into this.

Doug and Polly White's Let Go To Grow: Why Some Businesses Thrive and Others Fail to Reach Their Potential[2] is a look at what is needed at various points in growing a business, how one skill set (or executive) which is essential at point A, might be unneeded at point C ... and how the smart (and flexible) business owner can make these transitions.

The Whites are a couple who are principals in Whitestone Partners, Inc., "a management consulting firm guiding small and midsize businesses through profitable growth". Her background is in HR ("in people management and human systems"), while he managed to turn degrees in Physics and Engineering into a career in consulting and CEO and COO gigs in various companies. Here's their general over-view of what the book's about:

> Growing a company requires a very diverse set of skills, and you will face many challenges as your business matures. As a result, many businesses fail or stagnate well short of their full potential. Bright and hardworking business owners can sometimes figure out how to make the necessary transitions through trial and error. But, the trails can be hard and the errors expensive. By using what we've learned over the years about growing businesses, you can avoid many common mistakes.

For the book, they've come up with a way of classifying businesses, not so much on the money made, but by the functional structure.

- Micro Businesses – where the principal does the primary work of the business.
- Small Businesses – where the principal manages people who do the work of the business.
- Midsize Businesses – where the principal

manages the managers who manage the people who do the work of the business.
- Large Businesses and Conglomerates – this level is beyond the scope of the book, but this is where *"the principal has delegated P&L responsibility to a series of General Managers".*

The book is structured in four main parts, the first defining all this, the second looking at what's involved in running a Micro business, the third discussing taking a Micro business up to being a Small business, and the fourth looking at what's required to take a Small business to a Midsize business.

One might wonder why this starts with a focus on the micro business, but it's the first level where there are problems...

> It may sound like remedial counsel to say that before starting a micro business, the owner should ensure that he or she can do the primary work of the business. Yet, we ran into many people who … charged headlong into an entrepreneurial venture without thinking the issue through clearly. It is unusual for a startup business to succeed if the owner lacks the ability to do the primary work of the business.

An interesting element they introduce in this section is a 4-quadrant grid mapping urgency against importance, in order to figure out what to do in various situations, these work out as:

1. Neither important nor urgent.
2. Urgent but not important.
3. Both important and urgent.
4. Important but not urgent.

Each of these have 3-5 action elements, and several of those have multiple sub-points. One of the most useful of these (to me) was the second quadrant guidance to "use principles", which, once established set guidelines which made specific "rules" superfluous (one example was given to a young associate to judge what would or wouldn't end up on an expense report – if he'd be comfortable explaining to the legendary founder of his firm why a particular item was on a client's bill).

Let Go To Grow[3] is full of "case studies" where various companies the authors had worked with are given as examples (both positive and negative) for ways things could be handled. Obviously, in this space, it's difficult to present a lot of details, but I thought they handled goal setting with employees very well, a discussion of "the Peter Principle" and when not promoting from within becomes an option, and the importance of accurately and timely documenting systems and work flow in one's organization (something which we've recently been looking at in the start-up I'm working with) ... *"Once an organization reaches midsize, it requires documented processes to communicate to the organization how to execute specific tasks."* and *"When you identify better ways to do the work, you must change the process documentation to reflect the new reality"* stood out as particularly good points on this.

Obviously, a 250-page book is not going to be *encyclopedic* on a subject as wide-ranging as growing one's business, but I feel the Whites have done a very solid job of presenting most of the issues that one would face in taking a business from the smallest levels up into being a substantial entity. Anchoring it in the experiences of organizations that they've worked with over the years gives it a grounding that is both warning and inspiration (although rarely in the same story, unfortunately), with some finding just the right solution and others failing disastrously.

Oddly, Let Go To Grow[4] is not a *new* book, despite making it into the "Early Reviewers" program, having come out in the Fall of 2011. This means that there's less a chance of it being out there in the "brick and mortar" book vendors (heck, the link for the book on the publisher's site goes off to Amazon!), than usual, so your best bet is no doubt through the on-line big boys, who are offering it at about 25% off at this writing ... especially as this has not worked its way into the new/used vendors at any great discount. Needless to say, if you're not a reader of "business books", this won't have much to recommend itself to you, but if the subject of growing a company is of interest, this is a *very* good book on the subject!

Notes:

1. http://btripp-books.livejournal.com/145031.html

2-4. http://amzn.to/1MuTlal

Monday, August 5, 2013[1]

Movin' on up ...

This was another title that came my way through the monthly "Early Reviewers" program over on Library-Thing.com ... which more months than not pairs my library with at least one of my requests for books that have been offered by various publishers. It is *also* at least the third book that I have recently[2] acquired[3] via LTER[4] from the McFarland publishing house. As those keeping score at home may recall, I have been intrigued by this group, as their books are evidently targeted to the academic market (and so have extremely high cover prices), appear to be produced via print-on-demand (the covers have that tell-tale dimensionality of the plastic covering over the ink/toner), and, in the cases I've seen, appear to be "vanity" projects of various graduate researchers' papers. This volume, however, Skyscraper Facades of the Gilded Age: Fifty-One Extravagant Designs, 1875-1910[5], by Chicago-based architect Joseph J. Korom, Jr., is a true delight. While it may, indeed, be a labor-of-love "pet project" for the author, it is a remarkable look at the flowering of a certain type of building at a particular point in time, with the eyes of a specialist who can dissect the specifics of the architecture to a degree that the casual observer would have little chance of managing.

The book is a visual delight (for architecture fans, of which I'm one), chock-full of vintage (and some contemporary, shot by the author) photos of buildings, line art, Victorian advertisements, portraits of notable architects and financiers, close-ups of decorative elements, etc. This alone makes Skyscraper Facades of the Gilded Age[6] easy to recommend, but the text is also a pleasant surprise. This certainly *could* have been staid, dry, and "professorial", but if anything, it veers in the other direction, often exhibiting a floridness that echoes the buildings he's discussing.

> An architect's exact process of design is almost never evident to the casual viewer of the architect's end product. The final resolution of any architectural design problem has an infinite number of pathways to resolution, hence the varieties of resolutions – buildings – that surround us. Those who resided in America's great cities in the Gilded Age were surrounded, just as we are now, by an unbridled variety of building designs.

As one would gather from the book's sub-title, Korom takes a look at fifty-one buildings that were put up in the 35 year period around the turn of the last century. These are spread out across six sections which, to a greater or lesser extent, sort them into design categories. The chapters have evocative names: "Ways and Means", "Hopes and Dreams", "Togas and Parasols", "A Time for Funny Hats", "Towers, Dragons and the Stuff of Dreams", and "Eclectic Explorations".

Although he certainly isn't over-bearing with it, the author does have a bit of an axe to grind ... as a Chicago architect, he has an affinity for the famed "Chicago school" of skyscraper design, clean, unadorned lines, and powerful profiles ... so there is a certain amount of wondering what his predecessors were thinking in creating the mélanges of historical themes and stylings that were *de rigueur* in the "Gilded Age".

And what, you might well ask, is this "Gilded Age" thing? Korom helpfully addresses this:

> *The term "Gilded Age" was coined by none other than Mark Twain, one of the period's most beloved and admired novelists. Between pipe puffs and satirical anecdotes, this silver-mustachioed character of mythical Americana managed to produce, with the hand of editor, essayist, and writer Charles Dudley Warner (1829-1900), a piece entitled <u>The Gilded Age: A Tale of Today</u>. This novel, a product of 1873, satirized post-Civil War America by focusing on the nation's inequities, polarization, racism, materialism, corruption, and government graft. Various sources have cited the Gilded Age as one that spanned from the 1870s to the year 1900. Others, more persnickety, have pegged the period only from 1878 through 1889. Certainly, considering the novel's contents, any American period could suffice, with special honors given to the here and now. But for the purpose of this study, the Gilded Age's span of years applies to those from 1875 to 1910, since the social norms, personal values, and architectural aesthetics held in 1875 were, by and large, the same as those held in 1910.*

One of the things I found amazing here was how briefly some of these towers existed. A good number of them only stood for a few decades before being razed for newer structures. Frankly, I don't necessarily share the author's (and the great Louis Sullivan's) distaste for these buildings, and in many cases I feel cheated to not have been able to see these proudly standing in their respective skylines. However, I'm also thrilled that so many of the Chicago entries in the book are still there to look at ... and even had the serendipitous occurrence of being reading about one (1896's Fischer Building) on the bus, and getting off a half-block away to be able to ogle the actual item with fresh eyes of having just read its history!

Obviously, with various segmentations, and over 50 case studies, it's hard in the context of a review to take a meaningful dip into the descriptions involved. So, instead, I'm going to give you a rather long-ish excerpt here, which I think at least encapsulates the thrust of the book. From the intro to the second chapter:

The Gilded Age was a time of hopes and dreams. The hopes of the investment community were for wealth. The dreams of the architects were for fame. These were the forces that helped to drive buildings in America's cities higher than ever. Skyscrapers were singular achievements that were now clustered into groups; there were lots of them, and they were rising in both large and small cities, in towns, and in smaller towns. Like religion, jazz, or architecture, and to paraphrase Le Corbusier, skyscrapers, especially, were meant to "move us". America appropriated the skyscraper as a home-grown invention and even touted some as "proud and soaring things". The Gilded Age skyscraper symbolically allowed American to feel good about themselves and their achievements; after all, America was the heir to Greek democracy, Roman law, and Renaissance humanism. Virtues such as these deserved to be expressed by means of either wealth or architecture. Both investors and architects wished to make their mark, to leave something of themselves for posterity. One wished to do so with a brick of gold, the other with a brick of clay.

Our national identity derived not only from the ancients, as there were other design sources, other inspirations that entered into the country's collective consciousness. Tall office buildings helped to shape the nation's identity and these provided sources of regional and national pride.

American skyscrapers were diverse animals, creations that appeared in a multitude of styles; their forms were limitless and downtown America evolved into an architectural zoo. There were, though, many that defied any sort of neat categorization. Hybrids of hybrids sprung from the minds of educated architects, men well versed in the arts, cultures, and histories of that big, and old, continent across the Atlantic. Designing skyscrapers was challenging fun, and almost anything passed for serious work. Facades could include almost anything: angels, dragons, mythological creatures, animals, gods, goddesses, even nudes. Skyscrapers could rise to resemble castles, basilicas, chateaux, palaces, campaniles – almost anything dreamt of. It was an intellectual free-for-all that included combining these in any number of permutations.

Needless to say, if you're a fan of architecture, of that period of American history, or of the development of aesthetics, you will find a lot to love about Korom's Skyscraper Facades of the Gilded Age[7]. The one thing that most folks will *not* love about it, however, is its $49.95 price tag (for a sub-250 page book) ... the on-line big boys aren't helping here (Amazon is only knocking off 5% on this at the moment), but the new/used guys do have "new" copies at about 30-40% of cover – still steep, but in this case, probably worth it.

Notes:

1. http://btripp-books.livejournal.com/145278.html
2. http://btripp-books.livejournal.com/140721.html
3. http://btripp-books.livejournal.com/136286.html
4. http://www.librarything.com/wiki/index.php/HelpThing:Er_list
5-7. http://amzn.to/1U0WrVe

Tuesday, August 6, 2013[1]

"Mediators of energy-matter interaction."

I don't suppose that I should be surprised at having received this book from the LibraryThing.com "Early Reviewer" program … over the past 40 years I've no doubt read *dozens* of books dealing with the Chakras, in a wide range of contexts, cultures, and traditions. However, books from LTER[2] are always a bit of a "pig in a poke" … being things that one has indicated (usually based on a brief paragraph) that one might be *interested in* receiving, but rarely volumes that one has had a chance to look at, consider, or particularly want. Because of this I was very pleased with Shai Tubali's The Seven Wisdoms of Life: a Journey into the Chakras[3], as it is a reasonably well-crafted look at the Chakras, if from a rather "newagey" standpoint of personality typing, etc. Up front, the author states that he's focusing on the "psychological and transformative aspects" of the Chakras, and less on the "mystical and esoteric aspects", although as soon as he gets into defining things, he's smack in the middle of describing the *Nadis* (the 72,000 "energy channels" throughout the body), and *Prana* (the "vital life force" which flows through these), which is certainly more the latter modality than the former.

Here's a bit from his introduction:

> Man is not just flesh and bone. By saying that, I do not mean to support abstract and romantic ideas such as the soul. On the contrary, I mean to stress a whole realm of psychological dynamics, that may be invisible to our outer eyes but nonetheless are active all the time. Invisible is not irrelevant, just like atoms are a necessity in the total understanding of matter.
>
> There is another anatomy for man, a subtler one, which envelops the visible plain of the physical body like invisible sheaths. This anatomy is extraordinarily important both for the complete understanding of our psyche and for the realization of the further evolution of our consciousness.
>
> …
>
> In many respects, one may refer to this subtle anatomy as the anatomy of our psyche or, in an even broader sense, as the anatomy of our consciousness. The direct implication of this insight is that by understanding the depths of this anatomy, one may acquire a comprehensive map of one's psyche, through which one can navigate in a much more conscious way.

... that's a pretty good summation of where the author's going here.

Now, I suppose that there *are* folks out there reading this that don't know Chakras from Chuckles, so here's the short version (from me, not Tubali): Chakra is a Sanskrit word which means "wheel", which serves to describe particular energetic points on the (etheric) body where a "whirlpool" focuses particular types of energy, and are associated with colors, etc. There are generally held to be seven of these, 1st – in the crotch, 2nd – about at the bladder, 3rd – around the gut, 4th – at the heart, 5th – at the throat, 6th – between the eyes just above the brow, and 7th – at the very top of the head. Depending on the system/tradition these have specific functions and attributes, and The Seven Wisdoms of Life[4] presents the author's particular take on them.

In the second (main) part of the book, these are put forth as "The Search for – " the following:

1. Security
2. Joy
3. Power
4. Love
5. Communication
6. Wisdom
7. God

... with each of these having similar sub-sections dealing with the aforementioned "psychological and transformative aspects"... including:

- *Characteristic emotions and typical reactions.*
- *The type of trauma accumulated in the chakra.*
- *The chakra-oriented personality.*
- *Masculine aspects and feminine aspects.*
- *The "type of happiness" associated with the chakra.*
- *The "worldview" of the chakra.*
- *The "evolution of the chakra as it is reflected in the process of growth in a human lifetime".*
- *"Collective imprints" in the charka.*
- *The "historical phase in human evolution" associated with the chakra.*
- *Important interactions with other chakras.*
- *The chakra in "spiritual transformation".*
- *Recommended practices for aspects of the chakra.*

... there are also "polar emotions" focused at the level of the chakra, as well as "famous expressions" of the chakra personality type in terms of historical/mythic figures.

Again, this has a pretty significant "new age" lean to it, pulling from traditional systems to fit the "personality type"/psychological model the author has structured. To his credit, this seems to hang together quite well on its own terms. In the "Summary" section he discusses four ways to "extract wisdom" from the chakras … these include "higher wisdom", "spiritual practices", and "right actions", but one, "purification", sounded an awful lot like Scientology, with *vrittis* (a Sanskrit word that is literally "whirlpool", but means "disturbance of mind") standing in for *Thetans*:

> Purification is a therapeutic process, during which both body and mind are cleansed of psychological impressions and memories. These impressions appear in the chakras as vrittis – personality tendencies that reflect our deepest subconscious.

… but that's probably just me being snarky.

There are two appendices, one on "The Journey of *Kundalini* Along the Chakras", which gets heavily into the Sanskrit dictionary in describing how this is "the most important subtle force for the spiritual evolution of mankind", and one being "Questionnaires for Self-Evaluation", which includes two – a "Chakra Personality Type Evaluation", and a "Chakra Imbalance Evaluation". I, personally, found these worse than useless, but I'm the wrong guy to judge those sorts of things as they always irritate me.

Despite the latter points, I found The Seven Wisdoms of Life[5] a decent attempt at making a "newagey" system with "psychological and transformative" over-tones … not exactly a book I'd outright recommend as a *Chakra* book, but not bad for what it is. This is relatively new, so it might be bouncing around in the more new-age brick-and-mortar book mongers (which you should probably patronize if you wanted a copy of this, since the big on-line sources aren't offering much of a discount). Again, this wasn't exactly "my cup of tea", but it wasn't something I particularly disliked either … as is frequently the case (in the words of Dennis Miller) "your mileage may vary" on how this will appeal to you.

Notes:

1. http://btripp-books.livejournal.com/145565.html
2. http://www.librarything.com/wiki/index.php/HelpThing:Er_list
3-5. http://amzn.to/1VHg5HM

Wednesday, August 7, 2013[1]

Help Not Hype ...

I love *prizes*, and who doesn't? I won this book by being one of the first 200 people to register for the *"Content is Fire, Social Media is Gasoline"* webinar hosted by the good folks over at Wildfire[2] (which was quite interesting) ... although, given the subject matter, I suspect I would have eventually wheedled a review copy out of the publisher.

Overly attentive readers of this space will recall that I reviewed Jay Baer's previous book[3] here a while back, and, if anything, Youtility: Why Smart Marketing Is about Help Not Hype[4] is more in my wheelhouse, given the amount of blog copy and web content I crank out! On this point, his choice of Marcus Sheridan to write the Foreword was brilliant ... Sheridan was a pool installer who got hit hard by the economy-in-the-toilet phase that kicked in back in 2008 (and for some of us has never gotten any better), and had to figure out a way to *somehow* pull in new business, so turned to the Internet to search out marketing ideas. Of course, he found out a lot about blogging, in-bound marketing, content marketing, and social media, but the point of difference is that he pivoted *his* experience into a generalization:

> What I discovered ... is that consumers of all types expect to find answers on the Internet now, and companies that can best provide that information garner trust and sales and loyalty. Success flows to organizations that inform, not organizations that promote.
>
> ...
>
> My new plan ... was simple, I decided to act like a swimming pool consumer, instead of a swimming pool installer. I applied this methodology in two ways that changed my company and my life.
>
> First, I brainstormed every single question I'd ever received from a prospect or customer ... this list quickly grew to hundreds of questions. Then I answered every single one of those questions with its own blog post, adding hundreds of new pages to my website in the process.

Hundreds of pages. I can't tell you how many times I've been told by "sales guys" that you don't give the customer a lot of information, but here is a guy who *flooded* his prospects with info and turned around his business. He also found that if a customer read *30* pages on the site before a face-to-face sales appointment, the closing rate was around 80% ... in a niche where the average close is only around 10%. That's the difference that

"Youtility" makes – you become useful to the customer, and they trust your expertise, and you get the business. Sweet.

Baer takes stories like this and seeks to make a "system" out of it ... talking about "Top-of-Mind" awareness vs. "Frame-of-Mind" awareness, vs. "Friend-of-Mine" awareness ... where the latter is the more effective, and giving the example of the social media program Hilton runs which is focused on being helpful to travelers, without any specific promo involved for their properties, among several other widely varied examples. Of course, implementing this sort of program is hard in most corporate settings:

> *On the psychological front, the truth is that the tenets of Youtility – making your company inherently useful without expecting an immediate return – is in direct opposition to the principles of marketing and business deeply ingrained in practitioners at all levels. ... Youtility turns marketing upside down, and many businesspeople simply are not prepared ... In most companies, creating marketing that customers want is a colossal shift from the norm.*

Baer lists "three facets of Youtility", but notes that all three are rarely in every program, but there's got to be at least one of:

- *Self-Serve Information*
- *Radical Transparency*
- *Real-Time Relevancy*

There is some fascinating data in here ... when talking about the "zero moment of truth" (that instant when you hop online to research the option you're thinking about going with) he reports that Google says in 84% of cases this shapes the final decision ... and in 2010 the number of sources needed to decide was 5.3, while *one year later* in 2011 that figure jumped to 10.4 – a doubling of "data needs". Baer argues that we reached a tipping point this year, when 57% of Americans had smart phones (nearly twice the 31% of 2011), so *"It's worth taking the time to research {even} low-cost, disposable goods, because the friction and hassle of doing so has dropped almost to zero."*

Interestingly, much of the new "self-service" information gathering is no longer person-to-person ... actually contacting a person for info is the last resort (if videos and/or well done FAQs are available), and a study showed that consumers won't even *identify themselves* as a sales prospect until they'd independently completed 60% of the purchase decision ... heck, over the past few years the use of smartphones to *phone* people has dropped more than 10% while the volume of text messages has increased around 40%.

In terms of "radical transparency", the companies succeeding here are opening up levels of info that would have *horrified* those a generation back ... an example covered here is an amusement park that has prices for everything, from snack shop menus to gift store items, all spelled out on their web site so visitors can plan out their spending *in detail* well in advance ... another is the McDonalds Canada program of answering (in public) any questions about their food – in the first 7 months they'd answered 12,000 (out of 19,000) questions submitted. Here too, more is better ... *"companies with 101 to 200 pages generate 2.5 times more leads than those with 50 or fewer pages"* on their web sites, and *"companies that blog 15 or more times a month get 5 times more traffic than those that don't blog"* ... certainly a great argument for pumping out content!

As to "real-time relevancy", current trend lines show that the number of folks relying on mobile computing will surpass those on the desktop sometime in 2014, and Gartner forecasts mobile app downloads nearly doubling each year through 2016! Baer notes: *"Within a generation every customer and prospective customer of every company in every developed nation will have never known a world without the ability to access information at any time through a mobile device."*

The last section of the book is "six blueprints to create Youtility", which has a chapter each on the following:

1. Identify Customer Needs
2. Map Customer Needs to Useful Marketing
3. Market Your Marketing
4. Insource Youtility
5. Make Youtility a Process, Not a Project
6. Keeping Score

These start with paying attention to your social media chatter, and web analytics, and making an effort to get meaningful feedback from your current and prospective customers. Next you have to figure out how to be useful to your customers ... an example given here is of a knot-tying app developed by Columbia Sportswear, whose outdoor-loving customers may well have need of knots, but don't need to be beaten over the head with promos for the latest jacket.

Of course, nobody's going to use the app if they don't hear about it, so pushing one's Youtility efforts via all communications channels is important ... you're telling folks that you've got something to help them. Baer insists that helping has to become part of every company culture: *"You need to insource your Youtility program because just about every employee has useful knowledge locked in their head."* ... and making that accessible makes it useful. This also has to be a long-term course ... what your customers want and need today will probably be eclipsed by something new in a year's time, so the process needs to be on-going. And, finally, you need to have goals, milestones, and metrics in place that are able to tell you how you're doing.

I really enjoyed reading Youtility[5] and have already floated suggestions based on it to various clients and associates for their projects. This just came out last month, so should be out in your local brick-and-mortar bookshop that carries business titles, but of course the on-line guys have it at a discount (and the new/used vendors have "new" copies for less than half of cover) if you want to go that way. Good stuff here ... very timely and useful!

Notes:

1. http://btripp-books.livejournal.com/145689.html
2. http://www.wildfireapp.com/
3. http://btripp-books.livejournal.com/108780.html
4-5. http://amzn.to/1MuRSRV

Thursday, August 8, 2013[1]

Into Tibet ...

As I have frequently mentioned in this space, I am greatly enamored of the book section at the dollar store ... and used to be totally befuddled at how the nice hardcovers that one can get there found their way to the buck-a-copy shelves (they come from Walmart when they rotate out unsold stock, I've since been told). As you would expect (especially given my disinclination to read fiction), there's not *always* something there that I want, but every now and again I'll walk out with a couple of hundred bucks (at cover price) worth of books for well under $10 ... which is an *awesome* feeling! Of course, a key thing in play through this channel is that one is not particularly "invested" in a book that has only cost a dollar, so it invites a "what the heck" freedom to pick up something that, while sounding interesting, isn't necessarily on a subject with which I'm particularly familiar.

Which brings me to the current volume, Abrahm Lustgarten's China's Great Train: Beijing's Drive West and the Campaign to Remake Tibet[2] ... I'm not one of those with an inordinate fascination with trains (although I take the subway variety frequently enough), but I have read a great deal about Tibet, and China's interaction (oppression?) with that once-inaccessible land, so there was enough going for this upon a cursory examination to toss it into the shopping cart.

Perhaps I was coming to the book in just the right mix of interest and lack of focus, because I found it quite rewarding ... largely because its scope was rather wide, and depth – well, enough to get the main ideas across. This book is about trains, yes ... with enough detail in parts to make me glaze over a bit. This book is about Tibet, yes ... without spending too much time of the idea of the pre-conquest era, it contrasts the changes being brought to it with the world that living interviewees knew in their youth. This book is about China, yes ... opening a none-too-flattering window onto the vast, frustrating bureaucracy which runs that massive country. But this book is also about geology, topography, engineering, climate science, and what was needed to make an impractical vision into a functioning resource.

There are two main stories here, however, one about Tibet, and Lhasa in particular, and the *drastic* changes that the Quinghai-Tibet Railway has brought to this once sacred capital of an ancient Buddhist (/Bon) theocracy ... and the other being that of the dedicated engineers who made the seemingly impossible happen by tenacity, drive, and daring.

Being a long-time (informal) student of the Vajrayana path (I've been blessed to have been able to attend initiations by H.H. the Dalai Lama on five occasions), I find it *very* hard to address the cultural issues involved here dispassionately, and so I'm going to gloss over those to a large extent. Because the nature of the P.R.C., things in China are done a very particular way, and one of these is the insistence that all business, paperwork, exams, and *work* be done in Mandarin. The Tibetans speak various Tibetan dialects, and have had few resources to *learn* Mandarin, and wave after wave of Han Chinese have emigrated from the massively crowded coastal cities to seek their futures in the newly opened "western province" of Tibet ... taking all the jobs and benefiting from all the economic development that was promised as the result of building the railroad ... while the native Tibetans are progressively more marginalized in their homeland. Lustgarten has many interviews with residents of Lhasa, and villages along the path of the train, and the stories are heartbreaking.

Technologically, at least so far, the railroad is a triumph. The challenges of running rails through the Himalayas are, as one would expect, substantial, but the issues faced in establishing a stable route across the vast Tibetan plateau were perhaps even more daunting. Much of this landscape is "permafrost", but not in the sense that most folks would think when hearing the term, as the temperature in the region hovers around levels that allow for constant melting and refreezing, causing ongoing cycles of surging ground that frequently destroyed roads previously built to reach Lhasa.

If there are "heroes" in this book, it is the many engineers from assorted governmental agencies and universities who fought against the particular environmental quirks to come up with systems that would allow for a train to come to Tibet. Their solution was somewhat counter-intuitive, coming up with a system of "thermosyphons"(*"passive refrigeration devices that transfer heat against gravity"*), tall closed tubes that use a liquid such as ammonia or freon to circulate, carrying heat away from the ground. These were installed in long lines on the path the rails were to go, solidifying the ground sufficiently that other engineering approaches could successfully be put in place. There is some question regarding the planning models, however, and if "global warming" becomes a factor in the region, these may no longer suffice to keep the route passable.

This, naturally enough, brings up the issue of the P.R.C. bureaucracy ... this railroad was a vision of Mao, and it *was* going to get built, pretty much no matter the cost, and excuses were not something that anybody involved wanted to have to offer. Only the "rosiest" projections for environmental and construction models would be considered, and so the engineers had to both fight against a difficult geological situation, *and* one where those in charge were essentially demanding the impossible. And this doesn't even get into the incredible paranoia surrounding everything to do with Tibet in the Chinese government ... some of the incidents presented here (about, for instance, what is and is not permitted for passengers on the train), are truly bizarre.

I found China's Great Train[3] quite engaging, and the technological elements *fascinating* ... as noted above, if you have an interest in any of a wide range of topics, you'll likely find something appealing here. The book has been out for five years, but the on-line guys have it (at a 40% discount), plus the new/used guys (as is often the case once things have made it to the dollar store), have a bunch of *new* copies for 1¢ (plus, of course, the $3.99 shipping charge) ... so if you can't find it at the dollar store, that's your best bet for picking this up!

Notes:

1. http://btripp-books.livejournal.com/146051.html

2-3. http://amzn.to/1MuRqTA

Friday, August 9, 2013[1]

Didn't see it coming, I guess ...

Here's another one that I snagged at the dollar store. Generally speaking, if the book has to do with Tibet, I'll grab it, as that mountain kingdom has held an ongoing fascination for me, and I figure (especially at a buck), there will be something enough to hold my attention no matter what the specifics of the book are. However, I'm also a cynical guy moving towards full curmudgeon-hood, and there was a lot in Sabriye Tenberken's My Path Leads to Tibet: The Inspiring Story of How One Young Blind Woman Brought Hope to the Blind Children of Tibet[2] that I found more in the *"what were you thinking?"* zone than finding it "inspiring".

This is not to say that Ms. Tenberken's efforts detailed in her book aren't *admirable*, but perhaps the most amazing thing here is that she managed to succeed (heck, even *survive*) in her goals despite all the difficulties (anticipatable and otherwise) that were in her way. The author is from Germany, and is blind herself, although she did have dwindling sight up to when she was 12 or so (so is able to vividly envision things from descriptions), and at some point formed the idea that she wanted to start a school for blind children in Tibet.

She is evidently among those types for whom all travel is a grand adventure, as she describes numerous situations in China and Tibet hat I would have hated to have gone through during my globe-trotting days in my 20's and 30's, and she, with the complication of not being sighted, seems perfectly equanimical in the face of aggravations that would have turned me into the perfect example of "the ugly American"! The book opens with a description of her and a traveling companion on horseback, in the mountains, in a storm, attempting to find their way through, evidently without a guide, and then trying to get shelter in a village they encountered.

She then turns to story to a trip to Beijing, with its own matrix of frustrations, and a stay at Chengdu University. The tale eventually flips back to her preparation time in Europe. One significant achievement Tenberken had there was adapting Braille to the Tibetan language, requiring a conversion to a Latin-alphabet transcription of the Tibetan syllables. The system she developed was the key to her later efforts in Lhasa.

The narrative bounces back and forth between Asia and Europe, and one of the most unexpected snags she found was that she was virtually unable to find any funding ... her goals and many Tibetan development organizations seemed to be at odds, and every attempt she made to get government funding bounced back to her having to have backing from an established group ... she eventually got hooked up with a small one, but it ended up not helping her.

Undaunted, she ends up in Lhasa, and eventually connects with a family who ran an orphanage, who offered to build an extension for her school. This moves forward agreeably for a while, but it eventually turns bad, as these people end up embezzling funds that had supposedly been spent for furniture, etc.

To top this off, a magazine correspondent shows up to do a story, and works his way into their confidence, only to admit that he was in the country only on a tourist visa, and has drawn the attention of the Chinese authorities who suddenly pull the visas of Tenberken and her partner ... requiring them to journey to Nepal until they can get new approval for returning to Tibet ... not having funds to fly, they had to hire a driver, and the trip which typically took 2 days took 4 because of road conditions (forcing them to have to drive through a river where a bridge had failed).

Eventually they do get permission to return to Lhasa, but at that point the German organization that had been officially backing them pulled its support (it turns out the group's President hadn't been informing the board of anything happening in Lhasa, and was doing everything she could do to sabotage the project), and they were back on their own. Fortune smiled on them again, however, with another (quite well-to-do) Tibetan family offering them their large house and compound to set up the school again.

I suppose My Path Leads to Tibet[3] is inspirational in the way the author, despite everything, presses forward and eventually achieves her dream, but the path there is *brutal*, and it's difficult to read if one has any level of identification with her along the way. Except for the final turn of events, almost nothing goes right here, or at least not for long (before going horribly wrong). At several points (while dealing with German groups) the idea of her naivety comes up, and this certainly has an aspect of feeling like one of those "let's put a show on in the barn!" tales of cluelessness, but in this case including hazardous journeys, hostile governments, and people running scams left and right.

If you're looking for a book about somebody with seriously naïve plans overcoming a world of difficulties to make her "vision" come true, you'll probably like this book a lot ... however, if you're like me and cringe at people being idiots, this will be nails-on-the-chalkboard. It is one heck of a tale, though ... and certainly and interesting read. This does appear to be out-of-print (other than in e-book formats), but the new/used guys have "very good" copies for as little as a penny (plus shipping, of course), and "new" copies for a couple of bucks. This is more touchy-feely than I typically like, but I know I'm way off on the cranky end of that scale, so this would probably appeal to most readers more than it did to me!

Notes:

1. http://btripp-books.livejournal.com/146394.html

2-3. http://amzn.to/1MuQO0h

Saturday, August 10, 2013[1]

You sometimes wonder ...

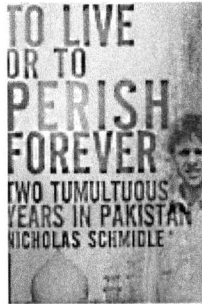

Yet another dollar store find, Nicholas Schmidle's To Live or to Perish Forever: Two Tumultuous Years in Pakistan[2] is a dense, fascinating read. Unfortunately, I'm getting around to reviewing it over a half a year after reading it, and much of the details have faded for me, leaving me with certain impressions, but not a lot of specifics still in my head. I had a couple of little bookmarks in there, which should have pointed me back to key passages, but upon re-reading those pages I'm not sure what I was intending there.

So, my apologies for this not being one of my better review efforts.

Schmidle's story is another of those that probably had better chances of ending with a bullet in the head than a book ...

> I went to Pakistan in February 2006, hoping to learn something about this troubled, nuclear-armed country, and about myself. I wanted to become a journalist, but most newspapers were closing their foreign bureaus, not opening new ones. And with next to no formal experience, magazine editors weren't exactly lined up outside of my door, eager to dish out international assignments. In the rapidly changing landscape of American journalism, it seemed the only way for an inexperienced hack like myself to try to make a name – and potentially a career – was by patching together fellowships and grant money, going somewhere newsworthy, and then praying for good luck.
>
> The Institute of Current World Affairs was my ticket. ICWA, as it is better known, is a foundation that sponsors two-year writing fellowships around the world. ... In June, 2006, the ICWA board selected me as a Phillips Talbot Fellow. ...
>
> I arrived in Pakistan by accident; my fellowship was intended for Iran. ... But shortly after the ICWA granted the fellowship, the people of Iran spoke, and chose ... a hard-liner whose vitriolic anti-American rhetoric dwarfed even that of his predecessors ... Overnight, the prospects of the Iranian government giving an American a two year-visa to ... write about the country's ethic problems seemed, well, pretty dim.

He managed to re-write his fellowship proposal for Pakistan (which has its own ethnic conflicts), and got approval from the foundation.

The years he was in Pakistan were particularly unsettled. Pervez Musharraf's Presidency was faltering, being threatened by the resurgence of Benazir Bhutto, and the whole country was thrown into chaos when pro-Taliban insurgents assassinated her.

And Schmidle was walking right into the middle of this. He'd been steered toward pro-Taliban leader Abdul Rashid Ghazi, who a Pakistani journalist suggested would likely be the leader of the country, were the Taliban come to power there. He'd managed to get introduced to an Osama bin Laden confidant who had been in the Pakistani intelligence service and airforce, Khalid Khawaja, who had previously been involved with Daniel Pearl's unfortunate attempts are penetrating the world of radical Islam in Pakistan. Remarkably, these chains of introductions worked, and soon Schmidle was bouncing around from one group to another, trekking across the country, and pretty much always being one wrong glance away from being summarily executed.

One thing he had in his favor (his physical attributes didn't help, being tall, blonde, and clean-shaven) was that he could speak Urdu ... and he was warned to, in nearly all situations, not speak English in public. A leader of one jihadi militia with whom he'd obtained a meeting *"considered Americans, Canadians, and all other 'crusaders' legitimate targets, but he saved most of his vitriol for Shi'ites"*, thereby fitting into the "ethnic conflicts" intent of his fellowship.

Frankly, much of the book is a whirlwind of Islamic personal and place names, with the author being handed off one to another, and the story arc blurs a good deal in the reading. However, his activities with the insurgents, naturally enough, draw the attention of the government, and he (with his *wife*, who was inexplicably along for the initial visit) get deported. Amazingly, he managed to get back into the country.

Some of the more memorable parts of the book are his journeys out of the capital and into the tribal areas bordering Afghanistan, or to the coastal region where Gwadar, a planned deep-water port (for some more stable time), is. For the tenuous position that he was in for most of his time there, the author does managed to cover a lot of territory, including a side trip to Bangladesh ... on one level To Live or to Perish Forever[3] is a bit of a travel book ... albeit one featuring a lot of Kalashnikovs.

An interesting data point that I did not previously know about Pakistan is that its name was an artificial construct from the 1930's, which came from P-unjab, A-fghan Province (North-West Frontier province), K-ashmir (which never officially left India), S-ind, and Baluchis-TAN ... making PAKSTAN, and "Pak" in Urdu means "pure", making the cobbled-together country name mean "land of the pure". Odd, but interesting.

At this point To Live or to Perish Forever[4] appears to be out of print, but the new/used guys have "new" copies for a penny (four bucks with shipping), so if you're looking for a rollicking adventure story full of exotic locales and Bond-like narrow escapes from chaotic environments, this is something that you should consider picking up.

Notes:

1. http://btripp-books.livejournal.com/146666.html
2-4. http://amzn.to/1MuQsqA

Sunday, August 11, 2013[1]

Watching others' searching ...

I guess I always need to learn things the hard way. A year or two back, when I'd been attending talks at the local Gurdjieff Foundation[2], I got into a discussion about the ever-expanding number of Fourth Way books out there, and was steered away from most on principle ... in that the majority of these "new" books were things that had never been intended for publication by their initial authors. However, their descendants (personal and organizational) saw these materials as having a certain market value, and had been variously going to print with them. Despite this warning (a very clear example of this is the recent collection of Madame de Salzmann's journals[3]), I've have plowed through a handful ... with little to show for it.

Like the de Salzmann book, John Pentland's Exchanges Within: Questions from Everyday Life[4] (material "Selected from Gurdjieff Group Meetings with John Pentland in California 1955-1984"), there is a sense of inappropriate voyeurism here. In the former, one has the "dirty" feel of having snuck off with someone's diary, and in this, well, it's a bit like going over security tapes (I hate to think of what was on the parts preserved from these meetings that did *not* make the cut for being "selected" for the book). Interestingly (to me, at least), *both* of these books were very difficult to slog through ... with my nodding off constantly while attempting to read them (this took me nearly *nine months* to finish ... a brutally slow pace), indicating something – I'm not sure if it's avoidance, or simply the lack of any "arc" across the material making it hard to keep up with.

Lord Pentland (actually Henry John Sinclair – of, I take it, *those* Sinclairs), had encountered the teachings of P.D. Ouspensky in his 20's, and spent the next couple of decades working quite closely with the Ouspenskys, even living in Madame Ouspensky's houses in the UK and America. Following Ouspensky's death (and a journey to India), he was introduced to Gurdjieff, and worked with him quite closely over the last year of Gurdjieff's life (1949). Remarkably (in that he was only a recent student), Pentland was tapped to head the Gurdjieff Foundation by Madame de Salzmann when it was established in New York in 1953, and he was President of the Gurdjieff Foundation of California from 1955 on.

I was unable to ascertain the exact situation in which the material of Exchanges Within[5] was accumulated ... I have to assume that these sessions were tape-recorded and later transcribed, as "live" transcription (*ala* a court reporter) would have been quite an undertaking, as well as a significant distraction. In any case, this volume covers the period from the establishment of the California foundation in 1955 to Pentland's death in 1984. The book is in three sections, 1955-1968, 1961-1977, and 1977-1984 (and, no, I don't have any idea why there's that over-lap between parts one and two). In these are chapters which contain from three to well over a dozen exchanges on particular topics, in the form of a person raising a question, and Pentland discussing the subject.

Again, the feel here is quite voyeuristic ... and somewhat without context. The vast majority of the questions are individuals wrestling with some aspect of The Work or another, but with very little information on what they're doing, how much they've studied, etc. ... and in most cases Pentland simply acts as a counselor, helping them to maybe re-frame what they're doing ... and perhaps provide actual *teaching* regarding that issue. The following is one such exchange, from fairly early on:

> QUESTION: In asking myself the question of who I am, it was as though I saw some symbolic representations through glass, having the feeling I am power, I am will.
>
> LORD PENTLAND: Not wrong. But not satisfactory. We all have experiences that we can call of a higher kind – the question is how do I act towards such experiences? It is what Gurdjieff's teaching is all about. These pose a question. What is the meaning of such experience in my life? Most of us don't face this question. We collect experiences like butterflies and pin them in a book and at the end have only a book of dead insects.
>
> Gurdjieff says man could be able to feel a relationship with everything around him, could actually be a part, play a part, of the surroundings. We see in respect to such experiences that we try to catch them, prize them. After a time, there is a satisfaction in having experiences – getting, then not understanding them – because experiences prove we are linked with something higher. We must understand our ordinary functions, which lead us to catching these experiences and pinning them in a book.

This is one of the more accessible/useful exchanges ... the initial question is reasonably coherent (many of these are "whiny", dealing with various things the person's not able to do or has not been able to achieve), and the response is pretty straight forward ... and there isn't any follow-up (frequently these float into a back-and-forth between Pentland and the questioner). Here Pentland deflects the ego-enhancing elements of the question and steers the attention to the *dynamics* of what one does with these. Many are no where near at this level ... as an example:

> QUESTION: I have a great opposition to being present. It seems like there's something that's stronger in myself that creates this feeling of "Don't be present, don't be present." It seems like my flying around with my imagination is a lot more fun.

Unfortunately, much of the book is Pentland taking this sort of thing and trying to turn it into something constructive (in this case he ended up doing several paragraphs about "attention").

At one point, very late in the book, Pentland does something that I really wish he'd done all throughout ...he takes a question (which was a long paragraph of prattling navel-gazing) and turns it into a chance to do some serious exposition on The Work ... several pages of really awesome focused text addressing key concepts ... here's how it starts:

> I would like to take advantage of your question and say something about the work on intention, which doesn't seem to have been brought into the work of the groups enough here, in my opinion. I think the work on self-observation is the best starting point and has been more or less received by all of you as the starting point for this work, and although there's a lot further to go in order that the idea of studying myself and observing myself might become fixed in me as an attitude, and although it's probably still not apparent to all of you how this idea of self-observation underlies the whole of the work as presented in In Search of the Miraculous, and even is constantly being referred to, both literally and metaphorically, in Beelzebub's Tales, still the work of self-observation and, beyond that, of receiving impressions of ourselves, hasn't been adequately brought into view.

... which is followed with a highly cogent detailing of things such as shocks at intervals in the octave, etc. I really, really, wish this book was more of that, than "peeping in the window" at the author helping to steer individuals along paths that are not ours, and for which we have very little info!

There is a lot of very interesting instructions dealing with The Work in here, but it's presented in such a manner that one has to sieve and sieve and sieve to find what is *generally* applicable out of what is specific to the individual questioner's situation. It is certainly an interesting *document* from the era following the deaths of Ouspensky and Gurdjieff, but one feels like a investigator going through innumerable hours of traffic camera videos, looking for particular pedestrians (or some such) while reading this.

If you are interested in getting a copy of Exchanges Within[6] this is a very good time as, while it is still in print (and so should be available from your local esoteric book seller), the on-line big boys have it (at this writing) for a whopping 79% off of cover price! I got my copy from the new/used vendors, but this is an awesome deal if it sounds like something you'd want to check out.

Notes:

1. http://btripp-books.livejournal.com/146898.html
2. http://www.gurdjieff-foundation-illinois.org/
3. http://btripp-books.livejournal.com/133926.html
4-6. http://amzn.to/1MuPXNi

Monday, August 12, 2013[1]

Exploring the Seventh Sense ...

I've been a fan of the work of Rupert Sheldrake for quite a while ... he's one of those guys who straddles the "metaphysical" and scientific worlds fairly gracefully, while being the target of a lot of attacks. You can't argue with his background, however, he has a Ph.D. in biochemistry from Cambridge, and is a research fellow of the Royal Society ... and he generally backs up his theories with as much practical research as can be mustered for things that are as slippery as telepathy. This one, 2003's The Sense of Being Stared At: And Other Aspects of the Extended Mind[2] is in many ways a follow-up to 1999's Dogs That Know When Their Owners Are Coming Home[3], taking the general outlines of the experimental structures there and applying them to human perceptions.

The book is set up in four parts ... Telepathy, The Power of Attention, Remote Viewing & Foreshadowing of the Future, and How Does The Seventh Sense Work? ... plus three appendixes, one detailing how to perform most of the experiments in the book yourself (which you can then report on at his website, Sheldrake.org[4]), one with notes and material used in the experiments, and a third on "theories of vision".

This latter is a key element in the book (as you would expect for something dealing with "staring"), as some of the ancient/early theories of how we see seem to fit the experimental data here better than the current model. Here's a bit on that from the end of the first section:

> Minds are connected through social fields. They also extend through attention, linking organisms to their environment. Our minds reach out beyond our brains and beyond our bodies every time we see something. ... vision involves a two-way process: an inward movement of light and an outward projection of images. Everything you see around you, including this page, is an image projected outward by your mind. These images are not inside your brain. Rather, they are exactly where they seem to be.
>
>   Through these fields of perception, our minds reach out to touch what we are looking at. Thus we should be able to affect things just by looking at them. Is this really so? The best starting point for this discussion is to think about the effects of looking at other people. If I look at someone from behind when she does not know that I am there, and

> *if she cannot tell I am looking by means of any normal sensory information, can she nevertheless sense that I am staring at her? There is in fact a great deal of evidence for a sense of being stared at ... {and} this aspect of the seventh sense has many implications for our understanding of human and animal nature.*

Now, you might wonder about the "social fields" mentioned in the preceding ... they are, essentially, *group* (pack, tribe, flock) versions of the "[Morphic Field](#)"[5] theory which Sheldrake is so identified. It is interesting that telepathic connections are almost always *strongest* between individuals who are already connected closely, and while these communications can't be explained by any *physical* interaction, the concept of there being an information matrix which informs the participants in that is not too terribly far-fetched.

Many of the experiments here arise from "common experience" sorts of happenings, knowing when a particular person is on the phone before you pick up, for instance. Sheldrake, however, takes the basic dynamics of these and structures experimental protocols to look into what quantifiable aspects there may be there. Some of the numbers are pretty amazing, with success rates in controlled experiments (on identifying callers) running from 40-65% where "chance" (in these tests) would be 25%.

Admittedly, a lot of the material in [The Sense of Being Stared At](#)[6] is a step above the dreaded "anecdotal", being based on surveys sent out to particular populations ... I guess this is fairly common in the social sciences, but it's not quite as "scientific" as situations where various levels of controls are in place. There are reports from several "laboratory" experiments as well, such as ones for the titular "sense of being stared at", which showed a 60-40 (%) split of correct answers when the subject *was* being stared at, compared with a 50-50 division of right and wrong guesses when *not* being stared at. While this is hardly earth-shaking, it is *significant* and certainly suggests there being something real involved in that perception. Interestingly, Sheldrake follows up the research in this area with a discussion of "the evil eye" in history and across various cultures!

Again, for most people unfamiliar with his work, the variously posited "fields" seem a bit of a stretch, but the author puts together a rather substantial defense of the concept, and while it's rather long-ish, I thought I'd put it in here:

> *Trying to understand minds without recognizing the extended fields on which they depend is like trying to understand the effects of magnets without acknowledging that they are surrounded by magnetic fields. No amount of chemical analysis of melted-down magnets could explain the way magnets affect things at a distance. Magnetic effects*

> only make sense when magnetic fields are taken into account. The fields exist both within and around magnets.
>
> Michael Faraday introduced the field concept into science in the 1840's. Fields are defined as "regions of influence". They connect things together across apparently empty space, and are responsible for many kinds of interconnection within the natural world. For example, the gravitational field of Earth stretches out far beyond the limits of our planet's atmosphere, and holds the Moon in its orbit. It is inside Earth, and also all around it.
>
> The electromagnetic field of the Sun affects all life on Earth, even though the Sun is 93 million miles away. The light and other radiations from the Sun are vibratory patterns of activity within the Sun's field, reaching out over literally astronomical distances.
>
> Many modern technologies also depend on invisible fields. Cell phones, for instance, would make no sense at all if they were simply material structures whose activities were confined to electronic circuitry inside them. They take in and give out information through the electromagnetic filed. There is both an intromission and an extramission of invisible influences.
>
> Unfortunately, modern thinking about the nature of the mind was shaped in the seventeenth and eighteenth centuries, when the only concepts available were those of matter in space, and spirit outside space. Most mechanistic scientists simply ignored consciousness, and consequently there was practically no progress in scientific thinking about the nature of the mind. And to this day the materialist-dualist debate has stayed stuck within the narrow limits of an outmoded way of thinking about matter.

I'm sure that Sheldrake would currently add the results of experiments that show that quantum entanglement (Einstein's "spooky action at a distance") as being part of the sub-atomic physical reality.

The Sense of Being Stared At[7] is a really thought-provoking book, and Sheldrake takes the reader from his animal experiments to some really fascinating theories for how "morphic fields" affect everything from planaria regeneration to the perception of "phantom limbs" and various more social elements. Oddly, this appears to be out of print at the moment, but new/

used copies can be had at various discounts. This is one of those that I wish *everybody* would read, as it has the potential of shaking some of the more staid world-views which need reconsideration ... so go find a copy!

Notes:

1. http://btripp-books.livejournal.com/147191.html
2. http://amzn.to/1FmVdOL
3. http://btripp-books.livejournal.com/52433.html
4. http://www.sheldrake.org/
5. http://www.sheldrake.org/Articles&Papers/papers/morphic/morphic_intro.html
6-7. http://amzn.to/1FmVdOL

Tuesday, August 13, 2013[1]

All over the map ...

It took me a very long time to plow through this one (and judging from other reviews I've seen out there, that's not an unusual complaint), and I'm thinking it's the book. Not that Murray Gell-Mann (a Nobel prize winner in physics) has written a *dull* book in The Quark and the Jaguar: Adventures in the Simple and the Complex[2], but it's one that delves into areas that are, perhaps, more specialized than the author might suppose. This is also one of the books that has been sitting in my "to be reviewed" stack for way too long, so I'm not coming to this with the freshest of commentary (sorry about that!).

The book is in four parts: 1 – The Simple and the Complex, 2 – The Quantum Universe, 3 – Selection and Fitness, and 4 – Diversity and Sustainability ... and most of those words are not used in the way you think they mean ... "complexity", "fitness", "diversity" all are based on really obscure mathematical theories and Gell-Mann jumps right into the thick of that in most of these, leaving behind (I'm guessing) most readers until he comes back out to the broad-stroke discussions.

The first part is particularly hard to wrap one's head around ... here are some cherry-picked section headings: "Complex Adaptive Systems", "Information and Crude Complexity", "Indeterminacy from Quantum Mechanics and from Chaos", "Context Dependence", "Conciseness and Crude Complexity", Algorithmic Information Content", "The Uncomputability of AIC" (see previous header), "Compression and Random Strings", "Random or Pseudorandom?", "Complex Adaptive Systems and Effective Complexity", "Falsifiability and Suspense", "Scale Independence", "Depth and Crypticity"... I suspect that you'd be surprised to find that, in the course of those, markets, sub-atomic particles, infants acquiring language, the predictability of place names, the inter-relation of chemistry and biology, etc., were all looked into in a reasonably lively manner.

The second part is pretty straight forward (OK, so as straight forward as quantum stuff gets!), but it's *dense* ... to illustrate this, take a look at this bit from the "Decoherence for an Object in Orbit" section:

> Say the object in orbit has mass M, the linear dimensions of the small regions of space are of order X, and the time intervals are of order T. The different possible coarse-grained histories of the object in the solar system will decohere to a high degree of accuracy over wide ranges of values of the quantities M, X, and T. The mechanism responsible for that decoherence is again frequent interaction with objects the fates of which are being summed

> over. In one famous example, those objects are the photons composing the background electromagnetic radiation left over from the initial expansion of the universe (the so-called big bang). Our orbiting object will repeatedly encounter such photons and scatter off them. Each time that happens, object and photon will emerge from the collision with altered motions. ...

... simple, right? Not too many pages after that he's talking Schrödinger's Cat, and then introducing his model of a complex adaptive system – IGUS – information gathering and utilizing system (which said cat could be argued to be), and thence into "Self-awareness and Free Will" (this is still in the discussion of quantum effects). Since Gell-Mann is the originator of the Quark, this heads off in that direction too, with discussions of [QED][3], [QCD][4], Gluons, Neutrinos, the varieties of Quark, assorted violations of symmetry, SuperString theories, stuff in the Planck scales, multiple universes, forward and backward time, etc. Fun stuff ... no, *really* ... it's always great to hear some guy who actually "gets" this stuff riffing on it.

You might expect that the "Selection and Fitness" part is where the titular Jaguar comes in ... well, yes and no. The chapters here go: "Selection at Work in Biological Evolution and Elsewhere", "From Learning to Creative Thinking", "Superstition and Skepticism", "Adaptive and Maladaptive Schemata", and "Machines That Learn or Simulate Learning" ... a lot of ground gets covered here! The author asks "Is There A Drive Towards Higher Complexity?", borrows terminology more familiar from Multiverse theories to look at "Fitness Landscapes", name-checks Dawkin's "The Selfish Gene", charts out chromosomal cross-over, considers population biology, talks about the "incubation" of ideas (the middle phase of Helmholtz's model), and "boundaries" of problems. The "Superstition and Skepticism" chapter is very interesting, although being, as one might have guessed, a bit skewed to the skeptical.

The last section is a bit of soap-boxing on the part of Gell-Mann, advocating actions and policies for both cultural and environmental diversities. While some of this is no doubt "evergreen", based on the material that precedes it, being a decade out at this point, there's been a lot of unanticipated change (or perhaps the absence thereof), which throws this off. There is a nice summation about where the book has been up to that point, however, which I think is useful:

> We have examined how simple rules, including an orderly condition, together with the operation of chance, have produced the wonderful complexities of the universe. We have seen how, when complex adaptive systems establish themselves, they operate through the cycle of variable schemata, accidental circumstances, phenotypic consequences, and feedback of selection pressures to the compe-

> *tition among schemata. They tend to explore a huge space of possibilities, with openings to higher levels of complexity and to the generation of new types of complex adaptive system. Over long periods of time, they distill out of their experience remarkable amounts of information, characterized by both complexity and depth. ... The information stored in such a system at any one time includes contributions from its entire history.*

Again, The Quark and the Jaguar[5] is not exactly an easy read, nor a particularly coherent one (in his efforts to pull so many things together, there is a quite a bit of jumping around), but it can't be said that it's not an *interesting* read, and it is bursting with data points that will surprise and amaze (I doubt there are a lot of readers out there whose knowledge spans what Gell-Mann has crammed in here). So, with the caveat that it's a good bit of a slog, I'd recommend this to those willing to expend the effort. Tellingly, this is still in print (perhaps it's used as a college text?), and the big boys have it on-line for a bit off of cover. However, since it has been out for a decade, the new/used guys have copies for as little as a penny (if I recall correctly I got *my* copy from either the Newberry Library Book Fair[6], or one of Open Books'[7] awesome "box sales"), so you can pick it up without too much of an investment.

Notes:

1. http://btripp-books.livejournal.com/147225.html
2. http://amzn.to/1FmUWLL
3. http://en.wikipedia.org/wiki/Quantum_electrodynamics
4. http://en.wikipedia.org/wiki/Quantum_chromodynamics
5. http://amzn.to/1FmUWLL
6. http://www.newberry.org/newberry-book-fair
7. http://www.open-books.org/

Saturday, August 17, 2013[1]

Mind-Body Healing ...

This was another interesting find at the dollar store ... and, as regular readers of this space appreciate, I do love picking up books there, both for the *obvious* reasons (a $24.00 book for a buck!), and for how they lend some degree of serendipity into my to-be-read stack. I suppose there's also the element of the "win" involved in finding a non-fiction title (that I am at least interested enough in to toss in the cart) amid the multitudes of fiction titles which make up those few shelves.

Stalkeresque readers will also recall that I've been involved in quite a lot of alternative health practices since my teenage years (back when dinosaurs walked the earth), including having studied with Peruvian shamans, trained in hypnosis, and other things along those lines. This, of course, made Dr. Rick Levy's Miraculous Health: How to Heal Your Body by Unleashing the Hidden Power of Your Mind[2] of immediate interest when I found it on the dollar store shelf ... and I want to point out (before I get into the caveats) that this is a very good book, that I would recommend, and which I wish I could find more (dollar) copies of to pass along to various friends.

That being said, I liked this book a lot more in the beginning than in the end. I was very excited when I read Levy's introductory material, including:

> I suppose I was uniquely prepared to expand the frontiers of mind-body medicine. I entered the profession of clinical psychology with the mind of traditional hard-nosed scientist totally committed to improving the human condition, a family mantle I inherited from my father who was a world-class biochemist and brain researcher at the National Institutes of Health. After I earned my PhD in Clinical Psychology, I held a number of traditional leadership roles that included chairmanships of the Departments of Psychology at two state hospitals ...
>
> By the late 1980s, I saw what the methods could do for people and realized their awesome implications for improving human wellbeing on a global scale. I became determined to get the methods out, even at the expense of my stature in the filed of psychology (at that time, the clinical use of meditation, hypnosis, and biofield energy work were considered "fringe"). I used to joke in those days that I was "a suit-and-tie guy working in the tie-dye field", but as it turns out, I was merely ahead of the curve. ...

Sounds *awesome*, right? Establishment shrink finds "mind-body" practices, and becomes a big advocate ... great story line. My excitement for the book only increased when the first two parts, energy work (a key element in the shamanic practices I'd studied) and hypnosis, were things that I was quite familiar with, and his presentation of these was solidly in line with my experiences in those areas. However, the narrative takes an abrupt turn following that when he shifts to meditation ... rather than being a suit-and-tie guy discovering these approaches in the course of his professional career, while at Brandeis University in 1966, he *"traded in {his} white shirt and tie for fatigues and long hair"* as so many did at the time, but

> The in 1969, Dr. Richard Alpert, now known as Baba Ram Dass, returned to the United States from a long trip to India to become one of the major teaches of Eastern thought and meditation in this country. ...
>
> I was fortunate to meet Ram Dass when I did. Not long after he came to Brandeis, he became a nationally known spiritual leader with thousands camped out daily on his father's estate to hear him speak. However, before his fame made him inaccessible, three or four of my classmates and I would spend a half day with him, listening to him talk and meditating together. Just by being in his presence, I felt my connection to something larger than myself. ...

Thud. The guy who in the late 80's *"realized {the} awesome implications"* of mind-body techniques, had been a personal student of Ram Dass, with 20 years of background (practice? He doesn't note how he carried forth his early experiences) in meditation. What a buzzkill.

Again, this does *nothing* to invalidate what's in the book ... it's just that the set-up was so fascinating, the story arc so promising, that finding that he *didn't* first encounter these healing practices in the course of a "hard-nosed scientific" career and become an enthusiastic convert to their clinical use but that this was a long-standing focus for him, sort of pulled the rug out from under my "cheering interest".

The book is in five parts: "Skill Building", "Self-Analysis", "Treatment", "Supplemental Methods", and "Preparing for the Rest of Your Life". The three approaches mentioned, energy work, hypnosis, and meditation, are the "tool kit" developed in the first part, and his exposition of these is excellent (which is why I've been eager to find more copies). The second part involves two sets of assessment tools, one conscious, with "scale of 1-7" queries, and one hypnotic which involved the chakras and "symbolic" representations (which, frankly, I found awfully literal – bodily complaints that correspond to cliché phrases or relations – heart disease from loss of love, eye problems from not wanting to see something, etc.). One of the on-going themes of the book is finding "the story behind the story" where you try to find the symbolic/mythic elements of your story.

One thing I should note is that there is a companion web site for the book, which includes a number of hypnotic inductions and guided meditations which he introduces in various sections. This is really an awesome approach, as many other writers in this niche would have those *for sale*, and making them available for easy download (and he even recommends burning them to CD) is very helpful.

Another thing I should note (and which regular readers of my reviews will no doubt find unsurprising), is that I have not "walked through" the process here. There are step-by-step elements for increasing levels of meditation and hypnosis, as well as all the assessment material, that I haven't delved into. The book is set up as a guide to daily practice, and I've not even attempted the first bits (although I'm certainly familiar with the general set of methods), so I really can't speak to how efficient/useful the program presented here is. However, there *are* things in here for combating stress, shifting modalities, and other specific issues, that I do *plan* to get into this at some point ... I have downloaded the audio files on my system!

I must admit that I have some doubt about the "story behind the story" approach, and especially with the surface-level symbolism involved in that ... but he describes many cases where the use of energy work coupled with hypnosis and meditative states has healed patients of his, so perhaps there is something there.

Miraculous Health[3] has been out for a while (5 years) and appears to still be in print (the on-line big boys have it for 30% off), but used copies (as one would expect for something that bounced out to the dollar stores) can be had for as little as a penny (plus the $3.99 shipping, of course). This is structured to appeal to pretty much everybody, and the instructional parts are both straight forward and reasonably comprehensive. I sort of wish Dr. Levy hadn't "broken the spell" of the pretense that he starts the book with, but that's a minor issue. It's one of the better books in this niche that I've read in a while, made all the better by providing the reader with those audio files.

Notes:

1. http://btripp-books.livejournal.com/147671.html

2-3. http://amzn.to/1HbMwn7

Sunday, August 18, 2013[1]

Talking to the wind ...

As I mentioned in a review a while back, I picked up a couple of Paulo Coelho's books as part of an offer ... and I'd, frankly, never heard of him or his books prior to that. I have since found that bazillions of people have read The Alchemist[2] and there is a large population of people who think this is metaphysical gold.

I can see now why Brendon Burchard is such a big fan, as his book[3] certainly is patterned on a similar idea ... contrived set pieces that are crafted to impart a particular bit of "wisdom" without, well, directly *communicating* it.

I must admit, I have never been the sort who gets much out of this type of thing ... just as I'd rather read Ouspensky's *In Search of the Miraculous* than Gurdjieff's *Beezelbub's Tales*, these "teaching stories" almost always (well, perhaps with the exception of Shah's various *Nasrudin* collections) leave me wondering why I and the author bothered to have that particular dance ... and I've come to understand that I just don't process symbolic stuff the way it's evidently intended to be taken.

Now, I try very hard to not go digging through other people's reviews before I write mine, but there were so many 1-star reviews on Amazon (not in relation to 5-star reviews, of which there are 8x as many) that I had to peek. I'm not as cynical about this as many of those commentators were, and I don't mind characters being "the this" or "the that", but this is more *Johnathan Livingston Seagull* than *Flatland*.

Of course, not being much of a fiction consumer, I'm faced with the quandary of just how much one should give away of the plot, characters, etc. ... there are folks over on the LibraryThing.com boards who are *rabid* in their hatred of "spoilers", to the extent that I wonder how fiction gets reviewed at all. The broad strokes, however, is that there is a shepherd in Spain, a former seminary student (so he's literate and reasonably educated) who has a series of encounters with various people who impart to him certain information or happenings ... all of which lead him further on in his search for a treasure that he saw in a dream. He ends up selling his flock, crossing to North Africa, getting sidetracked there for a while, going on a journey with a caravan (his vision was to take him to the Pyramids in Egypt), and meeting the titular (although not particularly central) character.

I found very little to bookmark in this, but there was one section that stood out ... probably because it is as close to a direct philosophic statement as is in the book:

> *He still had some doubts about the decision he had made. But he was able to understand one thing: making a decision was only the beginning of*

> things. When someone makes a decision, he is really diving into a strong current that will carry him to places he had never dreamed of when he first made the decision.

Throughout the story, the concept of "The Soul of the World" keeps coming up, along with one's "Personal Legend" ... but everything is vague, hazy, and round-about, and pieced out in dribs and drabs in the various scenes. Another element that bothered me was that there were all sorts of "loose ends" that were never dealt with ... but, again, I'm hesitant to spell out details that others might consider "ruining the story for them" ... certainly the penultimate twist to the story needs to go unsaid.

The Alchemist[4] was a pleasant enough read, and it flowed well enough that it didn't become bogged down at any point ... it's really not "my kind of thing" in general, but it also wasn't embarrassing or aggravating in its metaphysics, even if the ultimate "meaning" was vague. As these sorts of books go, this was a decent experience, and as "cardboard cutout" as most of the characters are, the writing was at least somewhat more expressive than (to pick a particularly egregious example) the "Celestine" books. Of course, if you're a fan of "teaching stories" or metaphorical fiction, or things along those lines, you're likely to find this charming, or possibly even inspiring (somebody came by as I was writing tonight and was all effusive on how much they'd liked the book ... as the late Johnny Carson put it: *"It takes all types to fill the freeway!"*, I guess).

As one might expect, given its cult-like following, this is unlikely to go out of print any time soon, and it's available in various editions. The one I have is being offered by the on-line guys at 40% off and used copies of previous editions/translations (oh, yeah – the original is in Portuguese, as Coelho is from Brazil) can be obtained for a couple of bucks. You won't be missing much not reading it, but there are a lot of folks out there who think it's great.

Notes:

1. http://btripp-books.livejournal.com/147901.html
2. http://amzn.to/1ddhLHs
3. http://btripp-books.livejournal.com/144832.html
4. http://amzn.to/1ddhLHs

Monday, August 19, 2013[1]

T-T-T-Talkin' 'bout HIS generation ...

I've been following Dan Schawbel since the days when I was actively penning The Job Stalker[2] blog over on Chicago Now, and had read and reviewed his previous book[3] a few years back. So I was pleased to have his current publisher, St. Martin's Press, send me a review copy of his new release: Promote Yourself: The New Rules for Career Success[4]. I've actually been "sitting on this" for a while, as the book showed up in early June, but the release date isn't until September 3rd ... I asked if they'd prefer to have the reviews come out closer to that time, and they said they would, so shifted it down the "to be read" pile a bit.

I must admit, I find Schawbel's books (etc.), frustrating ... and have been vocal about my disagreements on many particulars ... but it is pretty clear that these are based on "generational" factors rather than him being necessarily *wrong* in what he's saying. Schawbel has carved out a niche for himself, being the career guru for "Gen Y"/millennial workers, and what he writes is based in their worldview and the specifics of their evolving life cycle – while I'm coming to this as a crusty old "Boomer" (like most of the baby boom generation, I still have a very hard time imagining myself and my co-generationists as "old", but one doesn't have to go far – any recent pics of, say, Mick Jagger or Jimmy Page will do – to be presented with rather daunting evidence to the fact). One of the most notable elements in this book is how it very clearly addresses these differences ... there is a *fascinating* chart in here that compares Boomers (born 1945-1964), Gen X (1965-1981 – which does *not* include Billy Idol of the band by the same name – who is two years *older* than me!), Gen Y (1982-1993), and even Gen Z (1994-2010 – my kids' category) on a dozen attributes: core values, attitude towards education, mode of communication, management style, work ethic, form of entitlement, and view on job changing (among others). Most of these seem dead-on (how did he *know* that I primarily communicate via a land line?), and aside from the chart, he has sections "coaching" the Gen Y readers about what to expect in interactions with co-workers (supervisors) of other generations. It's amazing that it's as "foreign" as it is from both sides of that divide.

There were a couple of data points in the chart which were particularly interesting ... one being the *size* of these "generations" - there are 76 million "Boomers", 45 million "Gen X" folks, a whopping 80 million in "Gen Y" (especially notable as they represent the shortest span of birth years), and only 23 million in "Gen Z". Another set of numbers which is telling is "average tenure on the job before switching" ... Boomers stay 7 years, Gen X stay 5 years, and the average for Schawbel's Gen Y cohort is a paltry *2 years* (Gen Z is largely not in the workforce yet).

From the "Boomer perspective", Gen Y are the kids who grew up with "everybody gets a trophy" coddling, and so have very little perspective on what is actually deserving of reward ... the book doesn't shy away from this, though, and Marcus Buckingham presents this portrait in his Foreword:

> ... members of Gen Y are accustomed to constant, immediate feedback. Forget annual reviews; they want weekly or daily check-ins with their supervisors. And we know they're used to that feedback being overwhelmingly positive. They are accustomed to being praised for their uniqueness. The result is a challenging set of expectations. Nearly 40 percent of Gen Y ... {believe} that they should be promoted every two years. An even more eye-opening statistic: Only 9 percent believed that their promotions needed to be warranted by their performance.

Now, (I suppose, being a Boomer) I find much of Schawbel's advice here *incomprehensible*, much in the same way I found his earlier book occasionally delusional. He obviously takes the attributes of Gen Y as something to be accepted (and rewarded?) while most sound like *deep* character flaws to me. He encourages his readers to become experts in their specific niches (dismissing the generalist in favor of "one trick ponies"), and become "leaders" ... yet most of this has to happen within the first six months on a job – at which point the Gen Y kid needs to be either moving up to that corner office or moving on to the next gig. It's probably a good thing for Gen Y that they have Gen X as management buffers between them and the Boomers, because most of what is advocated in a "career development" mode here would make me never want to have any Gen Y people on staff ... zero loyalty, zero reliability, all "about them", and grossly unrealistic expectations of reward – an entire generation of mercenaries, single-skill cogs looking for the most accommodating machine.

Highlighting this was the section on "Intrapreneurship" - building entities within your current company's structure ... he has a list of factors, good and bad, about going this route, and the *attitude* that's reflected in these is somewhat horrifying:

> • ***Intrapreneurship allows you to create new positions and advance your career faster than you might have been able to on the regular track.*** The connections you'll make and the supporters you'll have behind you will allow you to potentially skip entire layers of the corporate hierarchy.
>
> • ***Intrapreneurship is less risky than being an entrepreneur because you'll have the corporation's resources available.*** If you're an entrepreneur, you could be financing your idea with credit cards or borrowing from friends and family. If the

idea goes belly-up, you could be out a lot of money and relationships could get strained.

• **Intrapreneurship can be a bridge to becoming full-on entrepreneur later on.** *By starting your own business on the job – on your employer's dime and time – you're gaining the skills, understanding of the process, and the confidence you'll need to run a business without your company's help in the future.*

Wow. Just wow. Is *everybody* "playing the system" these days? This stuff reminds me of "black hat" SEO – stuff folks do because they *can*, to hell with the ethics. It makes me think that there's a good reason the economy is going down the toilet!

OK, so that's my being "reactive" over this stuff. The book is actually full of some very good advice, *especially* for its target audience. Schawbel presents lists of various elements of one's career which are solid, and applicable across the generations, including a couple of dozen "soft skills" (and how 71% of employers value "emotional intelligence" over IQ), and a detailing of "leadership traits" which was very good. While the focus here is for everybody reading it to be a "leader" (and *all the children are above average* in Lake Woebegone – must be all those trophies), the specific job search and career growth advice is solid (I was pleased/amused that I was already practicing most of these in terms of on-line reading, networking, and skill augmentation – so it's not *just* for the millennials!). This is likely to be a very aggravating read for Boomers, but is no doubt a great resource for the Gen Y folks it was written for.

Promote Yourself[5] isn't officially coming out for another couple of weeks, but the on-line big boys have it for pre-order at a rather remarkable 40% off. This will no doubt be out in the business/career brick-and-mortars everywhere as soon as September rolls around. If you're in the target audience, you should probably pick up a copy … if you're not … well, it's sort of an anthropological study of a population that may represent what the future looks like.

Notes:

1. http://btripp-books.livejournal.com/148093.html
2. http://jobstalker.info/
3. http://btripp-books.livejournal.com/88138.html
4-5. http://amzn.to/1Kfa9BD

Sunday, September 1, 2013[1]

A personal journey into cultural change ...

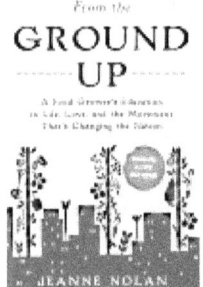

This one came into my hands via a slightly circuitous route ... my associate in the worm biz[2] had this recommended to him, and mentioned to me that it might be something that I'd be interested in reviewing. After having first contacted the publisher of *another* book with a *very* similar title (*oops!*), I got in touch with the good folks at Spiegel & Grau (a Random House imprint), and requested a review copy of Jeanne Nolan's From the Ground Up: A Food Grower's Education in Life, Love, and the Movement That's Changing the Nation[3], not really knowing much about it except that it deals with "the sustainable food movement" and how that's been developing in Chicago.

This is the sort of volume that might well be "irritating" in other hands ... it's basically (in its story arc) an autobiography, but one that serves as a seed bed for a florescence of in-depth information about many things Green. I really want to say "about urban agriculture" (an obvious interest of mine), but that would be misleading, as that is only a minor (albeit significant) aspect of the book, with the general thrust being for organic farming in various contexts. As frequent readers of these reviews will recognize, I tend to prefer books that "get to the point", but Nolan does such a skillful job of weaving the "industry info" in with her life story that they work as an ~~organic~~ whole (yeah, "ouch").

Perhaps what drew me in here as much as it did (far more than most biographical works) were certain parallels between the author's background and mine, from seeking out "counter-cultural" experiences in our teens to having worked with the late Abby Mandel (for whom I'd managed a PR project back in my early agency days, a *long, long* time ago) ... as well as hailing from the Chicago area.

The book begins with her return (with her toddler daughter) to her parents' home in Winnetka, IL in 2004, after 17 years of being part of the Zendik Arts Farm, an itinerant ecological commune (one that could easily be labeled a "cult", although it seems to have been more of a "cult of personality" around the founding couple who started the project in the heady days of 1969, but was still pulling in naïve yet earnest kids well into its fourth decade). She then details her early years, being a bright, promising class leader in her high school, until encountering a "tortured soul" boyfriend who incited a 180° shift in her attitudes and goals ... leading her to all-but dropout of school, and go off in search of a more meaningful existence than she saw being offered in sterile suburbia. She eventually encountered an ad for the Zendik group, and ran off to save the world.

One of the aspects that gives From The Ground Up[4] its gravitas and poignancy is that Nolan did *not* just run off for a rebellious year or two, but spent *seventeen years* as an integral part of the Zendik Farm, as it moved (seemingly at the whim of its leaders) from California to Texas to Virginia. Unlike other groups[5] (which were similar enough to assorted descriptions here that I had to Google "Zendik" to make sure it wasn't simply a euphemism standing in for a different organization) that had ranges of functions, it appears that the Zendik folks were primarily *organic farmers* ... if ones whose day-to-day existences and (familial and intimate) relationships were being micro-managed by group leaders ... so she had a LOT of experience with growing things in various environments when she found herself back in suburbia as a single mother with a high school education and no resume to speak of and a lot of shattered expectations of what she was "supposed to" have been.

It was her mother's wise request for her to start a garden on their property that started Nolan's new life. This enabled her to use those years of experience to create something impressive, and family friends (who happened to be on the board of Green City Market) mentioned that Abby Mandel was looking for an assistant ... a lead she followed up on, and eventually got the job. Green City Market[6] was the brainchild of Mandel, and is a continuing fixture of the Lincoln Park neighborhood, happening weekly spring through fall on the Clark St. facing of Lincoln Park, from its move there in 1999 to the present day. Nolan was not the ideal assistant for the project (having missed the "computer revolution" while being at Zendik), but *was* in the perfect position to take over the program that was associated with the Market across the way at the Lincoln Park Zoo.

Between the work on the demo "Edible Garden"[7] farm in Lincoln Park, and the gardens she was helping to develop for family contacts, the idea of starting her own business began to crystallize ... eventually materializing as "The Organic Gardener"[8], a service that would set up and manage organic mini-farms, initially out in the suburbs. She traces the growth of her company from the first few installations to such high-profile projects as the famed roof-top gardens of the Uncommon Ground restaurants, and setting up a vegetable garden for Mayor Emanuel's family.

Now, what I found most attractive about From The Ground Up[9] is how much *information* is woven through the biographical story-line. There are historical sketches of the organic movement, of urban farms and their predecessors (like how Paris used to have enough city lots producing fruits and vegetables that they not only provided all that the city needed, but were able to export the excess!), and descriptions of the leading lights of the assorted related movements, organic, urban, and small-farm, along with listings of resources. Also featured are many nuts-and-bolts issues like lead levels in the soil (from houses with generations of lead-based paints), sunshine necessary for assorted types of plants, and even what sort of fencing will keep out rabbits, deer, or (on city rooftops) those notorious moisture-stripping Windy City winds.

This is a mash-up of a personal story and an over-view of an evolving industry (along with a guide for where one can find what is needed to make these sorts of projects happen), in a reasonably seamless whole (the caveat "reasonably" here is due to her also adding on a very useful appendix,

"Ten Lists of Ten Essentials for every Aspiring Gardener", outside of the narrative). While much of the biographical material reads like a border-line soap opera (her personal life is "complicated", coming out of the Zendik world, but she manages to make it work to a rather remarkable degree), the depth and breadth of the agricultural material that is grounded by the life experiences she shares is worth the read for anybody interested in organic, urban, or alternative farming.

Of course, I *am* currently involved in the "urban agriculture" niche, so it is possible that I found Nolan's From the Ground Up[10] more exciting than somebody with only a passing interest in such things, but I'm recommending this "for all and sundry" for it being an engaging personal story that still manages to convey large chunks of knowledge about the emerging new agricultural movements. This has only been out a month or so at this point, so should be available at most better-stocked local book vendors, but the on-line big boys have it at a bit more than a quarter off of cover (it's presently only available in hardcover and e-book formats) if you can't find it at your handier surviving brick-and-mortars.

Notes:

1. http://btripp-books.livejournal.com/148394.html
2. http://natureslittlerecyclers.com/
3-4. http://amzn.to/1B6IVVI
5. http://btripp-books.livejournal.com/77773.html
6. http://www.greencitymarket.org/
7. http://www.theorganicgardener.net/edible.html
8. http://www.theorganicgardener.net/
9-10. http://amzn.to/1B6IVVI

Wednesday, September 11, 2013[1]

Sit down and shut up ...

There's a program that's been happening in Chicago for a number of years, where speakers (usually bearing newly released books) are featured in an early-morning event, called the Big Frontier. Sadly, today was the last of these ... at least in their original format. When I signed up to attend this, I sent a note to the good folks at McGraw Hill, asking if I could get a review copy of the speaker's book, and they managed to get that right out to me, and I managed to get it read in time for today's presentation. I had been torn between getting the review written last night, so that it would be out there for this morning's talk, and having the added context of the event for writing this ... which I opted for.

As one can tell from the sub-titles, Geoffrey Tumlin's Stop Talking, Start Communicating: Play Dumb, Be Boring, Blow Things Off, Lose Your Friends, and Other Counterintuitive Secrets to Success in Business and in Life[2] isn't your run of the mill communications book. The key concept here is the difference between what he defines as Higher-Order Communication (characterized by thoughtfulness and deliberation) and Lower-Order Communications (characterized by speed and convenience), with much of modern technology favoring the latter at the expense of the former.

Frankly, much of the book reads like a "weak Luddite" (to borrow a construction from "anthropic" classifications) plea for a return to lost values, despite the occasional insistence that the author really *really* likes all the tech that's making communications "bad". Here's a bit from early on in the book:

> Today, most of us struggle to have meaningful interactions because of the power, allure, and distractions of our digital devices. ... As personal and mass communication exploded in the digital age, essential interpersonal communications skills were left behind.

The skills of which he speaks sound like a fairly big order: *"listen like every sentence matters", "talk like every word counts",* and *"act like every interaction is important".*

Now, Tumlin is a "communications consultant", and much of what he's called to do is to "fix" things that are broken in various situations (often corporate, but also in other relationships), and there is a lot about Stop Talking[3] that is in the touchy-feely zone of a "relationship" self-help book ... encouraging the reader to "expect less from our devices" and "expect more from each other" ... looking at how communications can be misconstrued and how they can be managed. A key concept in this is "restraint and containment", where he suggests the "ABCs" of "Always Be Containing", and puts forth a list to "strengthen your restraint and build your communications conscience":

- Practice not talking.
- Delay your responses.
- Resist the urge to prove someone wrong.
- Eliminate witty comebacks, put-downs, and insults.
- Give yourself credit for the things you don't say.

Being a bit of a "bull in a china shop" (and a veteran of years of AOL chat room "flame wars" back in the day), this sounds like a recipe for taking all the *fun* out of the Internet to me ... but I suppose it is a guide for kid-glove handling of those with delicate sensitivities.

Speaking of the Internet ... Tumlin sorts things out into three realms of communication: Personal (*"What do I want to say?"*), Interpersonal (*"How will my message impact him/her?"*), and Mass (no control on individual impact). With the advent of the Internet (and escalated by Social Media) "personal" communications get blasted out as "mass" communications, creating chaos (if preserving a degree of "authenticity" - the author notes the fastest way for him to lose half of his client base would be to post items of a political nature on his social media channels ... although for many of us who have been on the web "forever", that's a horse that's long since left the barn, and I wonder where the self-editing stops, as it seems to be a constant spiral down towards a totally bland, sanitized, *inauthentic* public persona focused only on never making anybody uncomfortable!)*.

One thing that I wish the book included was a "cheat sheet" of the various lists ... there are a LOT of them in there, covering points for major elements such as de-escalation tactics, types of questions, tendencies leading to "communications inflation", "conversational shock absorbers", how to "play dumb", how to quit communicating with difficult people, how to suss out "identity issues" (before they blow up in your face), how to give negative feedback, etc., etc., etc., ... as well as the assorted acronymic bits and pieces. Stop Talking[4] is set up with sixteen "counter-intutive" statements (like "Be Boring") as chapter themes, each addressing some specific aspect of this approach to gaining control on communications. At times it feels like it's trying to be a "workbook" (with all the lists, etc.), but it doesn't quite get there, leaving the reader stuck between the *stories* of communications gone wrong, and the prescriptions on how to fix/prevent those sorts of problems.

Regarding stories, there are two types in here ... ones from the author's life in the military (he's a West Point graduate who served as a Ranger) and ones from his consulting work. The former are, generally speaking, charming, and bring a good focus on real-world communications issues (like when he scrubbed an exercise rather than expose his men to the potential danger of an unexploded claymore mine – and was initially berated for the decision), and the latter tend to be fairly horrific, with tales of really out-of-control situations (that call into question advice like "assume good intentions"!).

I realize that much of the above sounds like I didn't think much of Stop Talking[5], but it was an interesting read, with numerous clever turns of phrase that I wish I'd found a way to include in this review. I suspect that a lot of my problems with the book were *reactive*, being personally rather given to "verbal aggression" and other no-no's listed here (let alone thirty years of less-than-discreet Internet communications), and not anything particularly reflective of it. I suspect that those who are more "PC" in their interactions would not have the sort of issues with the book that I was encountering.

This has only been out a couple of months at this point, so is likely to be on the shelves of your better-stocked local book vendors, but the on-line guys have it for about a quarter off of cover price. If you have an interest in the dynamics of inter-personal communications, you'd certainly find a lot in this … but you may also find it a mirror that can be somewhat aggravating!

*At the talk this morning, Tumlin noted: *"Usually authenticity is an excuse for bad behavior."*, so it's clear where he comes down on that issue.

Notes:

1. http://btripp-books.livejournal.com/148596.html

2-5. http://amzn.to/1Lc5u0O

Sunday, September 15, 2013[1]

Outside of society ...

As I've mentioned (perhaps *ad nauseam*, your mileage will no doubt vary on that point), one of the joys of the book section at the dollar store (aside, of course, from the ability to get a new hardcover for *a buck*) is the enabling of serendipitous finds ... providing a certain "stirring the pot" to my reading. This was one of those "hmmm, this might be interesting" items tossed into the cart, and it proved to be a rather welcome departure from the mainline of my recent path through my to-be-read piles.

Rock & Roll Jihad: A Muslim Rock Star's Revolution[2] by Salman Ahmad was an interesting look into a Pakistani musician's life and career, with particular emphasis on how this played out against the unstable landscape of Pakistan's political shifts over the years. I found it interesting how much this dovetailed with another book I'd recently reviewed[3] (also a dollar store find), but from a wholly different perspective.

I don't know if I should be surprised or not at having never *heard* of the author here, or of the bands he's been in. While I listen to some "foreign" music, it's not exactly a passion of mine, and this was something that had never come across my radar. However, Ahmad, and his earlier band Vital Signs, and especially his later project Junoon[4] (which translates to "passion" or "obsession", and blends classic Sufi poetry and accompaniments with Rock sensibilities) appear to be a Very Big Thing (with over 30 million record sales) across the Islamic world, and in South Asia in general.

Frankly, while reading the book, I poked around a bit to see if I could find reasonably priced copies of the various CDs mentioned in it. I was surprised to find most were not even available via Amazon, even though having been released through affiliates of major labels. Poking around a bit more, I found that the band had dissolved (although continuing in name, but pretty much as a solo project, *ala* Andrew Eldritch's *The Sisters of Mercy*) in around 2005, with Ahmad continuing touring and recording with various fill-ins.

The fact that this book came out in 2010 makes me wonder if it's something of a "mid-life crisis" look back at the author's life ... with Ahmad trying to fit in his "rock star" status with his developing role in various NGOs and charitable projects. Getting ready to crank out this review, I went over to the Junoon.com web site, and was surprised to find that there was an *album* of the same name, timed to a common release with Rock & Roll Jihad[5], something that I'd not gotten at all from the book. I also noted that the site itself seems to have been largely abandoned, listing the ability to "pre-order" the eponymous album, due out June 1, *2010* ... although there were a handful of more recent "headlines" since then.

Salman Ahmad was born into an educated, mid-to-upper class family in Lahore, Pakistan, in the early 1960's. His father worked for the airlines, and the family moved around quite a bit as he was assigned to various offices worldwide. In the mid-70s they moved to the U.S., settling in to a suburban lifestyle in Tappan, NY, a short drive out of New York City. For the six years they lived there (something like Ahmad's ages 12-18) he absorbed a love of Rock music, learned to play the guitar, and started in with his first bands. The book, being primarily an auto-biography, traces his movements from his Pakistani birth to the US, and back to Pakistan for college.

Once back in Pakistan, his parents expected him to go into a career in medicine, and he attended the appropriate schools, and did, indeed, get graduated and certified as a medical doctor (as did his eventual wife, Samina). His passion for music, however, did not leave him, and he kept coming back to it.

The politics in Pakistan were not particularly amenable to his Rock vision ... and he was developing as a person and a musician just about the same time that fundamentalist Islam was gaining following (ala the Taliban). Early on he was playing at a party in a hotel when a Taliban-like group of fanatics burst in and, among other things, destroyed his prized guitar. This set up an attitude he maintained from that point forward, of finding ways to circumvent religious fanaticism when he could, be that in India, Bangladesh, Kashmir, Pakistan (under various regimes), or in post-9/11 America.

Ahmad's career was very much at the mercy of whatever forces were in power at a given time, under some, things blossomed (like when one regime championed Vital Sign's *Dil Dil Pakistan*), and under others (or even at different points in political rule, such as Benazir Bhutto's first embracing then banning Junoon) they were actively suppressed. One has to note, however, that he was quite lucky in the way that good fortune would eventually come along (such as Coca-Cola choosing one of his songs for the theme of the cricket World Cup), just when it was needed. Ahmad was willing to push the boundaries as well, taking the connections he'd made to create situations where it would be politically difficult to defuse his plans/shows (such as using the head of the local UN delegation to get word out about a concert event that was otherwise being blocked).

He worked these sorts of contacts remarkably well (and with fortuitous timing), getting to perform at the United Nations, and at the events around the Nobel Prize ceremonies, and was even made a UN "goodwill ambassador" for HIV/AIDS in Pakistan. As Junoon developed more into a personal project than a band, he also drifted into doing more charitable work, creating The Salman and Samina Global Wellness Initiative[6].

Again, Rock & Roll Jihad[7] is an interesting read, but it does leave one wondering ... especially if one takes a look around the web to try to connect the dots from the original Junoon's break-up to the present day ... at what he's been up to since putting out the book. This, of course, does not reflect unfavorably *on* the book (except to make one wonder how much "fictionalization" may have crept in to make the story flow the way it does).

Like many of the books I've picked up at the dollar store, this is still in print, and is available from the on-line big boys at very nearly full cover price (it's presently only 10% off). The new/used vendors, however (as one might expect) have "like new" copies for as little a 1¢ (plus shipping). I don't suppose that this is widely on the shelves of standard book stores (but could be ordered through them), so your best bet (if you can't find it at a DollarTree) would be the used channel.

As I noted, I was surprised that I'd not heard of Salman Ahmad or Junoon before picking up the book, but his is a very interesting story, and I'm likely to still try to find copies of his albums (there are some tracks on Pandora) … I have some friends who were quite enthused when they heard that I was reading the book, so I guess this is something that you might find appealing as well.

Notes:

1. http://btripp-books.livejournal.com/148932.html
2. http://amzn.to/1KeADTJ
3. http://btripp-books.livejournal.com/146666.html
4. http://www.junoon.com/
5. http://amzn.to/1KeADTJ
6. http://www.ssgwi.org/
7. http://amzn.to/1KeADTJ

Sunday, October 13, 2013[1]

A question of making ...

Back in July, I got a chance to attend the 3D Printing Conference & Expo down at McCormick Place, in the guise of my *other* blog, Green Tech Chicago[2]. Hod Lipson & Melba Kurman's Fabricated: The New World of 3D Printing[3] was very much in evidence at the show (they were selling it in the exhibit hall), not surprising as Lipson "programed" the conference part of the event. I noted that Wiley was the publisher of this, and shot an email their way requesting a review copy, which they graciously provided.

As a former publisher, I can imagine the difficulties of developing this book ... it's dealing with a subject, niche, and market that is *rapidly* changing, from constant new developments, to new players popping up, and other big names being swallowed up by competitors (one such consolidation happening just weeks before the show, leaving a "conspicuous by their absence" element there). Fabricated[4] attempts to take an in-depth look at a moving target, and one has to wonder how long this will stay relevant (I suppose they could update it on a regular basis, reflecting changes while building on the "historical" aspects here).

My *Green Tech Chicago* writing partner has opined that 3D printing is in the same place that computers were back in the early 80's, just emerging from the hands-on hobbyist phase and into the initial corporate expansion, but I'm not so sure. While I remember the limitations of my first computers, they pretty much did what I wanted them to do, within a time frame that I expected (boosted in my first PC by adding a math coprocessor!). One of the biggest issues that I see with 3D printing is their extreme slowness ... it may take 3-6 *hours* to print a desktop tchotchke, and folks I've talked to about this don't anticipate that available systems will speed up any time soon (due to limitations on the fabrication elements). This places a real limit on what can realistically be expected of the technology, as it means that the *machine* cost is spread out over a very limited population of printed items per year – especially if it's not running 24/7 ... if you're making "3 hour" items, you're going to have less than 3,000 if you *are* running the machine 24/7, and only around 1k if you're looking at a standard work day. If you're printing on a small "home/hobby" machine, that cost might not be too horrible, but if you're looking at a $40,000 pro machine, the cost per piece isn't going to make the doo-dads particularly attractive.

Now, sure, scanning and replicating *parts* that would be have to be hand-milled, etc., makes a lot of sense, but the "buzz" on the industry is pointing to home fabrication of *stuff*, and there are going to have to be some serious improvements on speed if that's going to work. This is one bit that was somewhat under-played in Fabricated[5], which tends to look at the "wow" and less at the "how" on the cost element.

This is not to say that it's not a fascinating read ... there are 14 chapters, each taking a look at a specific aspect of the 3D printing world. Now, for those of you who haven't seen 3D printing, here's the basic description from the book:

> *The way the 3D printing process works is as follows. The 3D printer, guided by instruction in the design file, squirts our or solidifies powdered, molten or liquid material into a specific flat pattern. After the first layer solidifies, the 3D "print head" returns and forms another thin layer on top of the first one. When the second layer solidifies, the print head returns yet again and deposits another thin layer on top of that. Eventually, the thin layers build up and a three-dimensional object forms.*

The systems vary, some using powder and an adhesive, some being glorified glue guns depositing plastic, some using lasers to fuse metal dust, or to solidify a gel, and even ones that use standard copy paper (printed, glued, and cut) to build up objects.

Aside from "object" printing (be it one-off replacements for machine parts, or "fashion" accessories), there are other realms that fall under the 3D printing umbrella: printed foods and printed body parts. Interestingly, the medical use of printer technology has been around for a while, as researchers discovered the ability to use old-school inkjet printers (which had less fine nozzles than later models) that could be re-fitted to spray out cells into sheets that could then be used on burn victims, etc., and scanning and "printing" bone replacements has come a long way and is now used almost routinely in some surgeries (with the obvious advantage of being able to make a scanned copy of one's existing bone, rather than having an "off the shelf" model that wouldn't fit as well).

Science fiction is a driving force in much of these developments, as people try to achieve what they've seen in that context ... but it's a long way from a 3D printer extruding cookie dough to barking orders like "Earl Grey, hot!" at a replicator. One of the "visions" in here is the concept of a robot that would "walk off the pad", having had all its component parts, its wires, its batteries, its sensors, as well as its mechanical parts, printed in one go. While current-tech machines can do some really remarkable things (entire mechanical structures with gears, etc., printed together and not needing subsequent assembly), the ability to do the whole thing is still a *long* ways away. A concept called the "voxel" comes into play here:

> *In the same way a pixel is a building block of an image, a bit is a unit of information, and an amino acid is a building block of biological matter, a voxel is a volumetric pixel (hence its name). The elementary units of physical matter are atoms. The elementary units of printed mater would be larger, a couple of hundred microns, the size of a grain of sand.*

> *Like a few colors on an artist's palette, a few voxel types can take you far. If fewer than two dozen element types gives rise to all biological life, a few basic voxel types can also open a large range of possibilities. To begin, let's combine rigid voxels and soft voxels. Using just those two types, of voxels, it's possible to make hard and soft materials. Add conductive voxels, to make wiring. Add resistor, capacitor, inductor and transistor voxels, to make electric circuits. Add actuator and sensor voxels and your have robots.*

While much of that is no doubt at least decades away, one area which 3D printing is creating massive new breakthroughs is in the plastic arts – sculptures, designs (they have a picture of a bottle opener[6] which is in the shape of a mathematical, single surface, "Klein Bottle") and even *shoes* that would be nearly impossible to produce if they weren't 3D printed.

Again, the book goes into a lot of detail in a large number of areas pertinent to 3D printing … so if you want to get caught up with this new field (or, at least caught up through 2012), this would be the book for you. Fabricated[7] has been out since February, so it's probably available at some better-stocked brick and mortar book vendors. The on-line big boys have it at a bit of a discount (20%), and some copies have gotten into the used channels, but you're not saving much there yet. Since the material here is so much in flux, I'd recommend getting this *now* (yeah, even if you have to shell out cover price), as it will give you the basics and a snapshot of things-as-they-are, before they get too changed … reading this in 5 years is no doubt going to sound "quaint"!

Notes:

1. http://btripp-books.livejournal.com/149203.html
2. http://www.chicagonow.com/green-tech-chicago/2013/07/from-the-3d-printing-conference/
3-5. http://amzn.to/1zBOCiC
6. http://www.bathsheba.com/math/klein/
7. http://amzn.to/1zBOCiC

Monday, October 14, 2013[1]

Revisioning marketing for the digital era ...

I actually "won" a copy of Gini Dietrich & Geoff Livingston's Marketing in the Round: How to Develop an Integrated Marketing Campaign in the Digital Era[2] following sitting in on a webinar that Gini was doing (they drew names of attendees). I actually know Gini from the local marketing scene, as she's head of the Arment Dietrich agency, and also has the "Spin Sucks" site[3] featuring her *Gin and Topics* blog. I've also been familiar with Geoff from "around the web", so I was coming to this book with a certain level of connection.

What I didn't expect, however, was that this slim volume was going to be a "whole approach" to marketing, but that's what it is. On certain levels it recalls Lon Safko's Fusion Marketing[4] in that it takes many disparate elements, previously "siloed" into their individual realms in the marketing mix, and setting them up in a new "marketing round" configuration, designed to fully integrate all aspects into an efficient whole.

> *Imagine your organizational structure as a wheel instead of a typical hierarchy. Think of marketing as the hub. The spokes are made up of public relations, advertising, Web, email, social media, corporate communication, search engine optimization, search engine marketing, content, and direct mail. They circle simultaneously.*

The book walks through the various elements and the pros and cons of their sub-sets in a very deliberate manner, with instructions for developing "dashboards", and specific exercises to do to get the details of your organization categorized for these approaches.

I found it interesting that much of the "theory" in the book is based on 17th Century samurai master Miyamoto Musashi's *The Book of Five Rings* ...

> *In the "Water Book", or the second ring, Musashi discusses five primary approaches to strategic engagement: the middle (or direct), above, below (the groundswell), and the left and right sides (combined to one: flanking). Independently or sequenced, the primary approaches form a baseline to approaching marketing strategies.*

These form the template by which the various activities are processed and planned, and set the tone for much of the discussion that follows:

> *When a competitor does something that draws significant attention or garners a lot of sales, it is natu-*

> ral to want to react, to mimic that marketing tactic. But that may, in fact, be the worst thing to do.
>
> Successful marketing capitalizes on your authenticity. It plays to your offering's strengths so customers will be more likely to buy. It is an expression of your culture, and its strengths and weaknesses. It is a measured response to you real and perceived competitors – a solution for stakeholders that empowers your brand to thrive regardless of competitor actions.

This goes to set up a case study, looking at the 2010 "Pepsi Refresh" program, which Coke did *not* respond to, and ended up expanding its lead by continuing its "authentic" activities. Each of the Musashi approaches are discussed, and the marketing elements set out in those contexts, and illustrated with case studies from various industries.

One interesting graphic here is a re-visioned "marketing funnel", which takes the "groundswell" approach – here the top of funnel is "awareness", followed by "consideration", followed by "conversion", moving into "loyalty", and finally towards "advocacy", which generates word-of-mouth, that then drives new customers into the top of the funnel.

Frankly, Marketing in the Round[5] could easily have been *twice* its 200 pages, but this has no "fat" on it ... and reading it is something of a firehose. I very rarely re-read books (within a few years of first reading), but this is one that I'm very tempted to take another run through, just to get the gist of it set better. This could also be spun out into a workbook. As noted, there are lots of forms and exercises to sort through marketing activities, and this could be expanded into a course. However, keep in mind, this is a book very much oriented towards either business owners or their marketing agencies, so it's not really a "for everybody" book ... but one that would certainly be of interest for anybody in those categories.

This just came out this summer, so should certainly be out there in the book vendors who carry business titles ... and the on-line guys have it at about 1/3rd off of cover. I found this a fascinating read, with a unique mix of contexts and approaches, and wish I was in a position to actually put some of this into practice!

Notes:

1. http://btripp-books.livejournal.com/149388.html
2. http://amzn.to/1dbC9ZI
3. http://spinsucks.com/
4. http://btripp-books.livejournal.com/143267.html
5. http://amzn.to/1dbC9ZI

Tuesday, October 15, 2013[1]

Or do they?

As regular readers of this space will no doubt recall, I am quite a fan of Scott Stratten, and regularly recommend his UnMarketing: Stop Marketing. Start Engaging[2] as an ideal introduction into the world of Social Media for those business folks who "don't get it". I appreciate his irreverence, and "outsider" stance on many things in the Social sphere (such as his insistence that the frequency with which one should blog is when one has "something awesome" to say ... which might well be once a month, rather than the three times a week that seems to be the "standard advice" out there). So, when I heard he was coming out with a new book, I shot an email off to the good folks at Wiley and requested a copy.

Now, Scott's been playing with the central conceit of QR Codes Kill Kittens: How to Alienate Customers, Dishearten Employees, and Drive Your Business into the Ground[3] quite a bit out there on the web, with kitties being featured in teases[4], and I had to wonder where the book was "coming from", considering his last book was rather rife with QR codes ... and (in case you were wondering) the QR code next to the worried-looking kitten on the cover *is* functional (I just fired it up with my phone), and leads off to a video of him riffing on the misuses of QR codes, much like those detailed in the book. On his web site, Stratten refers to this as *"a picture book, for fed-up business people"*, and that at least points in the right direction. This is a *very* quick read, under 200 pages, with LOTS of pictures, and everything focused on how social media marketing is regularly abused by the clueless.

Frankly, QR Codes Kill Kittens[5] reminds me of several other books. It obviously builds on the "unawesome" side of Stratten's The Book of Business Awesome/Unawesome[6], with it being a look at how QR codes (and other social elements) are being "done wrong". It also, largely in design (lots of pictures, tightly edited text), recalls Jason Fried's seminal Rework[7], and has a counter-intuitive title (if not carried through to the book contents particularly) similar to Jason Seiden's How to Self-Destruct[8]. The book has four chapters of about equal size addressing marketing or communications "fails": *They Don't Work*, *Nobody Likes Them*, *They're Selfish*, and *Your Time Is Better Spent Elsewhere*. One would think that this was all about QR codes, but it's really not, although they are a touch point to which Stratten does return. From QR codes in email (how does one scan that?), on highway billboards (how quickly can *you* launch that app?), in places with limited connectivity, heck, even on banners being towed by *planes* (pointing out that "motion and distance" are not particularly good for scanning, he notes *"I know one of you reading this approved the budget for it."*!).

A lot of the book focuses on Twitter foibles (horrible things that should never had gone out), lemming-like usage of display ads (a 50-character URL on a store's sign, a QR code sign placed directly behind a door's handle, making it unscannable, etc.), disasters of mobile site design, and assorted other levels of stupidity. Speaking of stupidity, here's a tasty quote:

> *Using an icon without an address leaves people to their own Internet skills and intelligence to find you.*
>
> *Never leave people to their own intelligence.*

… and you should *see* the "IQ test" that he suggests a particular spam e-mail is (asking you all your pertinent banking info, just to prevent having your "email closed" – reproduced on p.85).

If I had to voice a quibble on QR Codes Kill Kittens[9], it feels like it should have *more* about QR codes than it does – the title and chapter headings all point in that direction – while the unifying theme is actually more "things that kill kittens" across the board in social media marketing. And, while this is amusing in a *schadenfreude* way with all the bad behavior outlined (again, much like the "unawesome" half of Stratten's previous book), it takes a rather jarring turn on its last page … part of the "conclusion" section, where he veers into pitching his public speaking business. Call me a prude, but he could have moved the pitch to an "about Scott" section at the very end – there are 8 blank pages back there – which wouldn't have ended it on such a sour note (seriously, when I hit that "sell" paragraph on p.196, I suddenly felt like I'd just got done reading a *promotional* piece intended primarily for potential corporate speaking clients, rather than general readers … leading me to wondering if this *book* started out its life as a *brochure* for that market).

With that one caveat, I recommend this pretty much to all and sundry. Even if you're not in marketing, the "bad behavior" is funny enough to keep you reading. It's priced a bit steep for such a small book, but the on-line big boys currently have it at 40% off of cover, making it much more reasonable.

Notes:

1. http://btripp-books.livejournal.com/149630.html
2. http://btripp-books.livejournal.com/101421.html
3. http://amzn.to/1GhCjcJ
4. http://www.pinterest.com/pin/131026670382112400/
5. http://amzn.to/1GhCjcJ
6. http://btripp-books.livejournal.com/133717.html
7. http://btripp-books.livejournal.com/98114.html
8. http://btripp-books.livejournal.com/87069.html
9. http://amzn.to/1GhCjcJ

Tuesday, October 29, 2013[1]

How true? How real?

I must admit that I liked Paulo Coelho's Manuscript Found in Accra[2] a lot more than I did his previous mega-hit, The Alchemist[3]. I seem to have a limited tolerance for "teaching stories", preferring things to be set out directly, and find the vagueness of the genre extremely aggravating ... and at least here the structure's more discursive. The book, however, starts out with one of my pet peeves ... *don't* tell me something's "real" or "historical" if it's not ... and this is prefaced with a story, riffing off of the discovery of the Dead Sea Scrolls in Qumran, which purports to frame the book as being a manuscript discovered (in Accra) in 1974 by an English archaeologist, whose son Coelho supposedly meets in 1982, and who eventually sends him a copy in 2011 – the book being the transcription thereof.

The "manuscript" is a recording of a meeting happening the night before the French laid siege to Jerusalem in 1099, during the First Crusade, eventually killing most of the residents. This is focused on the heads of the three religions in Jerusalem, the Jews, Christians, and Muslims, plus another character, a Greek referred to as "The Copt", who is the central figure here. I am 99.95% certain this is a total fiction, given both the structure of the text, the references to alternate time lines of the various traditions, how the French are depicted, as well as how there are *clear* "borrowings" from other religious traditions unlikely to have been in play in 11th Century Jerusalem, and a general "new age" vibe across the whole ... but still it's presented as a legitimate archaeological discovery (even listing an export permission number from the Egyptian government to allow the discoverer to take it out of the country with him), which seeds an irritating wisp of doubt. Hate that.

The book is set up as a number of questions being asked by various residents of the city, a cross-section of society, all with differing specific concerns, each of which is answered by "The Copt" (oddly, only *his* answers are preserved by the individual supposedly taking it all down). So, the short review of the book would be "people in a city about to be massacred bring their existential questions to the wise men of the main traditions, and get answers from the other guy". Obviously, this does not make for a particularly illuminating review, so I'm going to pull stuff that I found interesting enough to bookmark, and we'll see where this goes.

First of all, "The Copt" is described as "a strange man" who left his home in Athens, and ended up settling in Jerusalem.

> He did not seek to join any particular religion, and no one tried to persuade him otherwise. As far as he is concerned, we are not in the years 1099 or 4859, much less at the end of 492. The Copt believes only in the present moment and what he

> *calls Moira – the unknown god, the Divine Energy, responsible for a single law, which, if ever broken, will bring about the end of the world.*

This, of course, is not expanded upon, but "Moira" is the singular of Moirai, "the fates" of Greek mythology, whose powers are generalized to the concept of "what's ordained", something that the Gods themselves can't avoid. I suppose that's a pretty useful place to be coming from if one's dealing with a population on the verge of being on the business end of a historic massacre.

One question is about "meaning", and there is interesting material here:

> *Others embrace the question, but since they don't know the answer, they start to read what was written by those who have already faced up to the challenge. And suddenly they find an answer which they judge to be correct.*
>
> *When that happens, they become the slaves of that answer. They draw up laws intended to force others to accept what they believe to be the sole reason for existence. They build temples to justify it and courts for those who reject what they consider to be the absolute truth.*
>
> *Finally, there are those who saw at once that the question was a trap; there is no answer.*
>
> *Instead of wasting time grappling with that trap, they decide to act. They go back to their childhood and look for what filled them with enthusiasm then and – disregarding the advice of their elders – devote their life to it.*
>
> *Because Enthusiasm is the Sacred Fire.*

This section goes on about madness, and love, and goals, and the Unwanted Visitor (death), and is quite inspiring.

One of the warriors, preparing to die the next day, asks *"What should the survivors tell their children?"* to which "The Copt" responds with a discussion of community, and various types of people and behaviors to be embraced or avoided. In closing a charming bit comes in:

> *Stay close to those who sing, tell stories, and enjoy life, and whose eyes sparkle with happiness. Because happiness is contagious and will always manage to find a solution, whereas logic can find only an explanation for the mistake made.*

And, to another question, coming from the unease of hearing battle preparations beyond the city walls, there's this:

> *Anxiety was born in the very same moment as mankind. And since we will never be able to master*

> it, we will have to learn to live with it – just as we have learned to live with storms.

This then shows how small worries build on themselves and eventually open the door to Obsession ... including some very familiar "type A" behaviors.

Towards the end there is a section would could have easily come from the *Mahābhārata*, where "The Copt" answers a question about the waiting enemies:

> The truly wise do not grieve over the living or the dead. Therefore, accept the battle that awaits you tomorrow because we are made of the Eternal Spirit, which often places us in situations that we need to confront.
>
> At such moments, set aside all futile questions, because they merely slow down the warrior's reflexes.
>
> A warrior on the battlefield is fulfilling his destiny, and he must surrender himself to that. Pity those who think they must kill or die! The Divine Energy cannot be destroyed; it simply changes its form.

At the very end, "The Copt" asks the evidently until-then-silent Patriarchs of the main religions if they have anything to say, and each gets about half page to do a little story, and the book closes with "The Copt" doing a very New Testament spin on having the survivors take this teaching out into the world. *Uh-huh.*

So, do you like "teaching stories"? If so, you'll probably *really* like Manuscript Found in Accra[4] ... as noted above, I found it more useful than Coelho's *The Alchemist*, but the whole "pretending to be real" (when I'm sure it's not) thing hangs heavy over this for me. It's a reasonably light, quick (under 200 lean pages) read, so it's not going to be something you'll get bogged down in. There don't seem to be any "cheap" options for picking up a copy, however, but since I got this it seems they've come out with a paperback edition, which might be your best bet. Given the popularity of Coelho's books, there's probably a good chance that you'll be able to find this at those few remaining brick & mortar book vendors too. Hey, I liked it well enough for what it is.

Notes:

1. http://btripp-books.livejournal.com/149982.html
2. http://amzn.to/1GhBZe9
3. http://btripp-books.livejournal.com/147901.html
4. http://amzn.to/1GhBZe9

Wednesday, October 30, 2013[1]

Speaking of which ...

This is another of those fascinating volumes that found its way into my library due to the serendipity of the dollar store book section. As is often the case with my "dollar store finds", this was unlikely to have been something that I would have picked up "at retail", but for a buck, the topic was interesting enough to get it into my shopping cart. As it was, it sat in my to-be-read stacks for nearly four years before I got around to plowing into it.

If I had one caveat to toss out up front about Anne Karpf's The Human Voice: How This Extraordinary Instrument Reveals Essential Clues About Who We Are[2] is that it is *very* British. Karpf is an English journalist and BBC broadcaster (and author and sociologist and university professor), and a lot of this has that very prominently in-grained in terms of descriptions (how many Americans would describe a vocal pattern as "posh", for instance?) and references (lots of TV and radio programs I'd never heard of). To be fair, this is no doubt how the rest of the world feels when hitting a U.S. book that's rife with cultural references, but it stood out enough that it occasionally was "an issue" with how I was absorbing the info.

Also, for being a book that I quite enjoyed, it ended up with nearly no little slips of paper for places that I felt I needed to return to, either for choice bits for this review, or for "future reference", which is odd ... especially given that this is not a "light read", for a book with 300 pages of text, The Human Voice[3] carries an additional 80 pages of notes (in a considerably smaller font size than the text) – so you would *think* that there would be notable factoids that I'd have marked.

To be honest, there's a certain *obsession* here ... as though this topic was one that has been a long-time preoccupation of the author. There's a breadth to the survey that's almost more than most folks would want to know, but all presented clearly and significantly annotated.

Because I don't have specific notes to pull from here, I'm going to fall back on a crutch that I feel I use too frequently, but which does give the reader at least the "30,000ft view" of the scope of the work ... breaking it down by chapter headings. This is in three (untitled) sections:

> PART ONE
> 1. What the Voice Can Tell Us
> 2. How the Voice Achieves its Range and Power
> 3. How We Colour Our Voices with Pitch, Volume, and Tempo
> 4. What Makes the Voice Distinctly Human
> 5. The Impact of the Mother's Voice (even in the Womb)

6. Mothertalk: the Melody of Intimacy
7. The Emergence of the Baby's Voice

PART TWO
1. Do I Really Sound Like That?
2. How Our Emotions Shape the Sounds We Make (and Other People Hear Them)
3. Male and Female Voices: Stereotyped or Different?
4. How Men and Women's Voices Are Changing
5. Cultural Differences in the Voice

PART THREE
1. From Oral to Literate Society
2. The Public Voice
3. How Technology Has Transformed the Voice
4. Voiceprints and Voice Theft
5. How People and Corporations are Trying to Change the Voice

Obviously, that's a LOT of info that Karpf has condensed here. Again, I'm guessing most folks have *not* even read moderately on the subject of the voice, and assorted research that deals with it, so the book is pretty much a non-stop flow of *"wow ... who knew?"* moments. Some examples from early on: *Newborns prefer to hear their mother's voice filtered in the way that it would have sounded to them in the womb. ... {Babies} can pick out their mother's voice from other voices well before they're able to distinguish her face from other faces.* ... although by age 4 most have switched to visual modes. Also, whereas males will talk "baby talk" to children under 4, by the time they're 5 most males will use "adult speech" in addressing children, while females still maintain the specialized forms.

There are fascinating elements of how vocalization has changed through global communication. There is a "vocal fashion" called HRT – the "high rising terminal" - *"in which the intonation of questions is applied to statements"* that *"seems to have begun in New Zealand, moved over to Australia, migrated to American teenagers (especially female), and eventually colonized Europe"* ... however, its spread (particularly to non-teens) is likely to limit its lifespan, as it has lost its "cool" factor. The author also deals with issues raised with Indian call centers ... it appears that callers from the UK have even a *worse* reaction to heavy accents than their US counterparts ... but as one call center trainer notes: *"It is very challenging to unlearn their natural manner of speech."*.

There's a good deal about how TV presenters and politicians have had to concentrate on adapting their voice for optimal effect. While some of the cases here (Margaret Thatcher, Tony Blair, etc.) are familiar enough to be useful examples for the US reader, there are a lot of names, evidently well known to the UK audience, that I certainly had no reference point to go on. However, I'm guessing the "cultural differences" here only become an issue in 15% or so of the book, so, given the massive amount of material here, that's not a particular problem over-all. There is a lot of psychological stuff here too, such as: *The voice both reflects and mediates our relationship with the outside world, and can be used to express attitudes and feelings that would be derided or dangerous if articulated through words.*

The Human Voice[4] does still seem to be in print, with the hardcover being a "bargain price" and less than a third what they're asking for the paperback (!). One would think, given that this has gone out to the dollar stores, that there'd be cheap copies via the new/used vendors, but not so much that you'd be saving a lot with the added shipping in that channel. If you have any interest in the voice, I'd say this is a good bet ... it's a fascinating collection of info on the subject.

Notes:

1. http://btripp-books.livejournal.com/150253.html
2-4. http://amzn.to/1FifsvG

Saturday, November 2, 2013[1]

Celebrity reading ...

OK, so I have to admit, the *main* reason that I picked up Craig Ferguson's American on Purpose: The Improbable Adventures of an Unlikely Patriot[2], was to read up about his old band-mate (and new 12th incarnation of the Doctor) Peter Capaldi. Who would have thought, back when they were in the Glasgow punk outfit The Dreamboys, that one would be an American late-night TV fixture, and the other would be in the most iconic of UK television characters?

As regular readers of this space will sense, while I'm *open* to reading biographies/autobiographies, they aren't a major segment of my library ... although they can be a welcome break from the "same old same old" if I've been in a bit of a rut (and those Social Media/Marketing books just keep on coming), and this was a *delight* to read. While the book is hardly self-congratulatory (frankly Ferguson beats himself up quite a bit here, with what seems to be reasonably unfiltered looks at his past), judging by it Ferguson has got to be either one of the *luckiest* guys on the planet, or simply smashing *brilliant*.

While I watch him fairly regularly (his talk show is right about in that overly-late hour that I think about getting something to eat for dinner, so am kicking around in the kitchen with the TV on), I've hardly followed his career. I knew him initially from the old Drew Carey show, and am familiar with his on-line @CraigyFerg persona, but I had *no idea* of all the stuff he's been involved with. He has written and starred in a number of movies (most notably, *Saving Grace*, but has had roles in vehicles as disparate as the classic English sci-fi romp *Red Dwarf* to the voice Owl in *Winnie the Pooh*), he's penned a well-thought-of novel, and has built up a solid stand-up comedy side-line. Very little of this is actually detailed in the book ... just the major projects (well, some minor TV things – that I'd never heard of – are in there too for their "narrative advancing" properties), which gives the impression that he sort of "stumbled" into success ... when he was actually working quite a bit more than one would get from just this.

At least half of American on Purpose[3] is Ferguson dealing with his inner demons, from his pudgy "outsider" youth, into his punk band years (there's a pic of him in this which totally channels Sid Vicious at his most drugged out), and into his forays in various aspects of show business. Ferguson was a hard-drinking, hard-drugging knock-about, but evidently with enough talent to keep getting acting, comedy, and related gigs. Much of the first two thirds of the book are the arc of him from birth to sobriety (he quit drinking in February 1992), including his break-through into a certain level of fame following his "Big Hitler" comic success in the 1986 Edinburgh Festival Fringe. As a recovering alcoholic myself, I was able to intimately relate to Ferguson's struggles with chemical dependence, and that is a key element of the story being told here.

The over-all arc of the story, as one might infer from the title/sub-title combination, is a bit of a love letter to America. In his youth, Ferguson had a chance to visit the U.S. with his father, who he told (while up in the old observation area in the crown of the Statue of Liberty) that he'd live in America one day. While I can be as jingoistic as any Constitutionalist looking out at the insanity of other parts of the world (or even Washington D.C.), it's refreshing to see Ferguson's take on the U.S. and our culture. He gives a very touching illustration of what he sees in America in a baseball analogy ... in that you can totally *fail* seven out of ten times, but if you keep getting back up to bat, and succeed just three out of ten times – you'll be in the Hall of Fame (i.e. with a .300 batting average) ... that plus not having the long-festering sectarian divisions that so mess up older cultures.

One thing I found a bit odd in American on Purpose[4], and this is, I suspect, a bit of his "telling tales on himself", is that he goes into a lot of detail about his various personal relationships – including several failed marriages. Now, I have no way of knowing just how *representative* the ladies he discusses are (they might be just the tip of the iceberg, if they follow like his acting credits here), but he deals with each in detail, and makes a point of having a photo of each in the picture section. I don't know why this struck me as odd, but I was wondering what purpose that served ... was it just a way to do a more significant "shout-out" to his exes, or was this some sort of back-hand bragging (all of them are quite attractive)?

Again, I really didn't know what to expect when I ordered this (I picked up a used copy of the hardcover over on Amazon for 1¢ plus shipping), but it is a nicely balanced, funny, touching, and eye-opening book (some of the stories of his working with Johnny Carson's old producer are fascinating). Its main arc is that love-letter thing, but with clear sub-arcs of his substance problems, his love life, and his career. The book ends with him heading back to Scotland at Christmas 2008, as his mother was dying ... and did so soon after he was able to visit her in the hospital. He has a chance to frame the rest of the book with a wander around his old haunts and a coming to grips with his being Scottish *and* American ... a very emotionally satisfying note to end on.

American on Purpose[5] is still in print in paperback and ebook editions, so is likely available in the humor sections of the larger brick-and-mortar book vendors (as wells as via download), but, as noted, "like new" copies of the hardcover are out there in the new/used channels for as little as penny – so you don't have any excuse for not snagging yourself a copy if this sounds like something you'd like to spend a few hours experiencing. It's hard not to be impressed with Craig Ferguson after reading this, because his story sure can't be all about luck.

Notes:

1. http://btripp-books.livejournal.com/150334.html
2-5. http://amzn.to/1e9fGMX

Sunday, November 3, 2013[1]

Groping towards security ...

This is another book that I got via the LibraryThing.com "Early Reviewers" program. If you're not familiar with the LTER, it allows site members to put in requests for review copies from a list of a hundred or so books being offered by publishers that month. Each book has a certain number of copies, and there are typically five to ten times (or more) the number of requests than the number of available books. This is where the "Almighty Algorithm" comes in ... a complex mix of factors that connects the offered titles with readers who will, hopefully, be the best match. This has proven to add yet another source of variability in my reading, as I typically win *something* every month.

I am very pleased to say that Permanent Emergency: Inside the TSA and the Fight for the Future of American Security[2] by Kip Hawley and Nathan Means was one of the more interesting, engaging, and well-written books that I've gotten via LTER (which does tend to be a bit of a "pig in a poke"). Needless to say, that is *not* what one would expect of a book which is, at its most basic level, the story of the development of a government agency. I'm going to be referring to Kip Hawley as "the author" here, as he is the person brought in to the Department of Transportation to help develop the Transportation Security Administration, and so this is *his* story, but I strongly suspect that the readability and pacing of the book are the work of co-author Nathan Means, which has me considering looking up some of his other titles.

Permanent Emergency[3] features an interweaving of two narrative threads, one being in Washington, with the development of the TSA, and one internationally, with the evolution of the terrorist threat. The book starts with the chaos of 9/11, with the DOT, FAA, FEMA, and the military trying to find out what was happening and what they had to do. There is a section recapping that prior to Hawley being pulled back to D.C. ... he had been a Transportation advisor in the Reagan administration, a Vice President at Union Pacific Railroad, and was an executive with a Silicon Valley transportation supply-chain software venture when Secretary of Transportation Norman Mineta's staff convinced him to come on board to help build the new organization.

Obviously, everything had changed in a moment about flight safety ... after decades of the "standard procedure" being to cooperate with hijackers because they were likely to have the plane land some place they could collect a ransom and disappear, it was now evident that new players were in the game, and were looking to rack up maximum body counts ... any way they could. Following the 1988 cargo-hold bombing of Pan Am flight 103 over Lockerbie, Scotland, most attention was directed in things being checked on the flight, but following 9/11, everybody going on board a plane was now having to be considered a potential threat.

Hawley paints a picture of an on-going cat-and-mouse game with the terrorists on new technology. Some of these will be instantly familiar … the attempted "shoe bombing" that has an on-going legacy of having to go through security checks unshod, and the "underwear bomber" whose attempts to set off a chemical mix in his drawers raised an entire different set of concerns. There are a LOT of "odd rules" that have been in place over the past decade or so which get explained here. For instance, the "3-1-1" rule – 3oz bottles, in a 1qt ziplock bag, 1 bag per passenger – is based on the study of the various chemical mixes that the terrorists were using. The 3oz size proved to be too little material to be able to efficiently mix an explosive (even though they had to admit that the answer to the question of "could multiple terrorists mix their individual sets of liquids and make a bomb?" was a somewhat disconcerting "maybe").

One of the on-going "technical" threads here is the development of explosives based on hydrogen peroxide – one of the key liquids of concern. Fortunately:

> *The hydrogen peroxide formula was extremely sensitive to minute variation, meaning that a spilled drop made a difference in whether or not it would work. Even with a world-class laboratory, the success rate in mixing the formula was around one in three. In addition, the fluid was dangerously corrosive and would cause severe burns if exposed to skin, not to mention that it had a strong pungent odor that would attract attention in airport secure areas …*
>
> *… the baggie took al Qaeda's explosive of choice off the table for aviation attacks, obviating years of their research and development and pushing them to consider less effective bomb formulas.*

Further technical advancements (like a device that can "sniff" even microscopic particles seeping out of containers) have led to the easing of these rules over time.

In 2005, Hawley becomes TSA Administrator and is thrown in to the deep end of the intelligence world … one thing that he implements, while not quite up to the Israeli model, are "BDOs" - Behavior Detection Officers, based on a program independently started by Paul Maccario at Boston's Logan Airport.

> *The BDOs were trained to refer to a sheet that scored various behaviors – distress, fear, fidgeting – on how alarming they were. BDOs used a cocktail of targeted emotions that drive the point-based system. By weighing different behaviors on a score sheet and confirming that they observed multiple alarming emotions, BDOs were able to incorporate*

> a more objective approach to what is perceived to be a very subjective technique. Every day in America 2 million people walk onto planes from every possible ethnic, religious, cultural, and racial background. The score sheet was meant to provide some sort of threshold before selecting people for additional screening or questioning, and hopefully protect us and the passengers alike from mistakes driven by preconceptions of what a terrorist looks like.

There is also a significant amount of material here about Hurricane Katrina, as the agencies involved in the terrorism fight also were pulled in for that. Especially inspirational was how the Air Marshals were able to be mobilized from postings all over the country to act as key "first responders" keeping order at airports in the affected area.

Frankly, both sides of the story are sufficiently complicated and detailed that I really can't do justice to them in this review, but Permanent Emergency[4] follows both with the tenacity of a good spy novel. There is obviously a lot of stuff we're *not* being told, but the amount of information here is really remarkable. Very useful, also, are sections at the end listing the names of all they key players (on both sides), and page after page of organizational acronyms, going into what they stand for and what those organizations do … fascinating stuff. There is also a time-line from 9/11/01 through 07/01/10 when a new permanent TSA Administrator was put in to replace the author.

Permanent Emergency[5] just came out this summer, so is likely still out in the bookstores. It's available in hardcover, paperback, and ebook, and the on-line big boys have it at about a quarter off of cover price, which might be your best bet for picking it up since it hasn't seemed to have filtered down to the used channels to have a substantial discount (when individual shipping's added). I found this fascinating, and think it would appeal to anybody who likes spy thrillers, and books about politics.

Notes:

1. http://btripp-books.livejournal.com/150726.html

2-5. http://amzn.to/1ETT7SR

Monday, November 4, 2013[1]

A man of wealth and taste ...

Needless to say, this is another of *those* books ... something picked up to fill a gap in an on-line order between what I have in the cart and where free shipping kicks in, and simultaneously filling a gap in my otherwise rather expansive liberal arts education. While I'm a bit upset that the on-line guys have raised the bar for free shipping from a $25 order to a $35 order (meaning fewer orders and more contemplation on what needs to be in there), I assume that these Dover Thrift Editions of literary classics will always come into play in getting right to that level.

I'm guessing that *everybody* is at least generally familiar with the Faust story in its various permutations. I was surprised to read in the introduction here that Christopher Marlow, whose Dr. Faustus[2] was posthumously published in 1604, had based it on an earlier work that was supposedly about an *actual* person, a *"German astronomer and necromancer who died about 1540"*. A contemporary of Shakespeare, Marlow is credited with having expanded the range of expression in English composition in his brief career (he lived only six years past his graduation from Cambridge in 1587). This is the classic tale of the Magus who makes a "deal with the devil" for worldly gain ... in this case by obtaining the services of one Mephistophilis.

I'm always fascinated to see how material like this leaches into popular expressions of religion. Like George Bernard Shaw had *his* Satan say in *Don Juan In Hell* (act III of *Man and Superman*): *"The Englishman described me as being expelled from Heaven by cannons and gunpowder; and to this day every Briton believes that the whole of his silly story is in the Bible."* and one wonders just how much of the Christian "back story", as believed by its less educated adherents, derives from passage such as:

> FAUSTUS:
> So Faustus hath
> Already done; and holds this principle,
> There is no chief but only Belzebub,
> To whom Faustus doth dedicate himself.
> This word "damnation" terrifies not him,
> For he confounds hell in Elysium;
> His ghost be with the old philosophers!
> But, Leaving these vain trifles of men's souls,
> Tell me what is that Lucifer thy lord?
>
> MEPHISTOPHILIS:
> Arch-regent and commander of all spirits.
>
> FAUSTUS:
> Was not that Lucifer an angel once?

MEPHISTOPHILIS:
  Yes, Faustus, and most dearly lov'd of God.
FAUSTUS:
  How comes it then that he is Prince of devils?
MEPHISTOPHILIS:
  O, by aspiring pride and insolence;
  For which God threw him from the face of Heaven.
FAUSTUS:
  And what are you that you live with Lucifer?
MEPHISTOPHILIS:
  Unhappy spirits that fell with Lucifer,
  Conspir'd against our God with Lucifer,
  And are for ever damn'd with Lucifer.
FAUSTUS:
  Where are you damn'd?
MEPHISTOPHILIS:
  In hell.
FAUSTUS:
  How comes it then that thou art out of hell?
MEPHISTOPHILIS:
  Why this is hell, nor am I out of it.
  Think'st thou that I who saw the face of God,
  And tasted the eternal joys of Heaven,
  Am not tormented with ten thousand hells,
  In being depriv'd of everlasting bliss?
  O Faustus! Leave these frivolous demands,
  Which strike a terror to my fainting soul.
FAUSTUS:
  What, is great Mephistophilis so passionate?
  For being depriv'd of the joys of Heaven?
  Learn thou of Faustus manly fortitude,
  And scorn those joys thou never shalt prossess.
  Go bear these tidings to great Lucifer:
  Seeing Faustus hath incurr'd eternal death
  By desperate thoughts against Jove's deity,
  Say he surrenders up to him his soul,
  So he will spare him four and twenty years,
  Letting him live in all voluptuousness;
  Having thee ever to attend on me;
  To give me whatsoever I shall ask,
  To tell me whatsoever I demand,
  To slay mine enemies, and aid my friends,
  And always be obedient to my will,
  Go and return to mighty Lucifer,
  And meet me in my study at midnight,
  And then resolve me of thy master's mind.

> MEPHISTOPHILIS:
> I will, Faustus.

Now, Dr. Faustus[3] is a *play*, and so there are various scenes with characters coming and going, some played for humor, some for horror (or at least moral discomfort), and some no doubt the "F/X" of their day (as Mephistophilis provides numerous marvels). Things, of course, do not go well for Faustus at the end, and we see him counting down the final minutes before he's taken off to hell, becoming increasingly more panicked at the prospects:

> O, no end is limited to damned souls!
> Why wert thou not a creature wanting soul?
> Or why is this immortal that thou hast?
> Ah, Pythagoras' metempsychosis! were that true,
> This soul should fly from me, and I be chang'd
> Unto some brutish beast! All beasts are happy,
> For, when they die,
> Their souls are soon dissolv'd in elements;
> But mine must live, still to be plagu'd in hell.

As you can tell from these excerpts, the language has changed somewhat, and in some places it's a bit less than flowing to the modern ear (although nothing like trying to work through Chaucer, writing a couple of centuries earlier), and there are a few footnotes defining words (or Latin phrases), no longer in common use. Interestingly, this Dover edition is explicitly available to use in theatrical presentations – which would be an interesting way of encountering the material.

While the Dover Thrift Edition of Dr. Faustus[4] is very much in print, the odds of finding it in any brick-and-mortar bookstore is pretty slim as the *cover price* on this is a mere $2.50 – making it ideal for padding an order to get to free shipping, not so much for convincing a retailer to get it in for the pocket change they'd make on it. Also, while there are "new" copies for as little as 1¢ out there, you'll have to add shipping to that, so if you can't convince you local book monger to have one sent out, adding this to an order with the online guys is no doubt your best bet!

Notes:

1. http://btripp-books.livejournal.com/151014.html
2-4. http://amzn.to/1GhAMUb

Saturday, November 9, 2013[1]

What's not to like?

I actually "won" won this book ... back in February author Dave Kerpen was the featured speaker at the Big Frontier meeting, and there was a contest for the most "live Tweeting" from it. Since I tend to be a clicky-clicky fool at these things, I ended up winning, and getting copies of two of his books. This one, Likeable Business: Why Today's Consumers Demand More and How Leaders Can Deliver[2] is the first one of those I've gotten to so far.

Kerpen got into the "likeable" business early on ... in college he got a job at Boston Garden and Fenway Park, as a snack hawker and on his first night he sold a mere 12 boxes of "Crunch & Munch", which really wasn't going to do it for him.

> I decided later that night that while it was fun being at games, I wanted to at least make a decent living hawking Crunch 'n Munch. So, my second day, I put some passion into my work – a little singing, a little dancing, a little screaming, and a lot of goofy Dave. I sold 36 boxes, three times as many as the first night. I stepped up my efforts for the rest of the week. The thing is, I'd be the first person to admit that I had no real talent as an entertainer. My only asset was passion, and perhaps fearlessness. I began to scream at the top of my lungs each night in a effort to pull attention away from the game people paid to see and towards the buttery toffee popcorn with peanuts I was selling.
>
> Passion paid off. Within weeks I had developed a persona as the "Crunch 'n Munch Guy", and regulars began to take notice. The in-stadium cameramen liked my schtick and began to feature my goofy dancing on the large-screen Jumbotron during time-outs. After the Boston Herald published its first article about me, fans actually started asking me to autograph boxes ... At my peak, I was selling between 250 and 300 boxes per game and making, with commission and tips, between $400 and $500 a night – an excellent living for a college kid.

Aside from Passion, Kerpen proposes "11 Principles of Likeable Business" here, which serve as a structure for the book, which features chapters on each of the following:

1. Listening

2. Storytelling
3. Authenticity
4. Transparency
5. Team Playing
6. Responsiveness
7. Adaptability
8. Passion
9. Surprise and Delight
10. Simplicity
11. Gratefulness

Each of these ends with a section of "Social Tools and Principles" for that list item, plus a handful of suggested "Action Items" to begin to apply the chapter's insights in one's business. He also makes a Maslow-esque "Likeable Pyramid", but while the list of principles are in there, they don't build in order, with numbers 1, 2, 8, and 5 across the bottom level, 9, 6, and 10 across the second level, 3 & 4 (combined) and 7 on the third level, 11 on the fourth level, and "likeability" (with his cribbed-from-Facebook thumbs-up icon) at the apex ... it's interesting, but I'm not sure it actually *adds* anything aside from a branding graphic.

Each chapter has numerous suggestions and case studies. One thing I found fascinating in the "Listening" chapter was this exercise:

> *... go to Twitter.com and enter into the search bar the name of your company, product, or category. If you work for a large company, enter the name of your company and the words "I wish". ... You'll find lots of people talking right now about you, your competitors, your products, and your services.*

This is in a section that's bookended by stories of how Build-a-Bear has thrived by listening (including a "Cub Advisory Board" made up of kids), and of how Blockbuster failed because it *didn't* listen (to customer dissatisfaction over late fees).

As regular readers of my reviews will recall, I "have issues" with those who advocate a squeaky-clean purged-of-all-controversy on-line presence. It's no surprise, then, that I found Kerpen's approach to "Authenticity" refreshing. In this he suggests:

> *As you develop your online persona, be sure to convey your in-real-life self in your digital presence. Learn to embrace the lack of boundaries between personal and professional and online and offline.*

He further personalizes this with a statement about how *he* would react to the different approaches when hiring a candidate:

> If two equally qualified job applicants were placed in front of me, one with a completely open Facebook profile with drunk photos displayed for the whole world to see and the other with a blocked account, I would choose the open one. Being authentic requires a willingness to share your true self with others.

He later adds:

> Inauthenticity is cumbersome, ineffective, and, ultimately, a losing proposition. Because of the nature of the web and social media, along with the fact that everything is open and spreads, people need to know that the person they're speaking with is genuine and "for real".

I was surprised to see that Kerpen was able to quantify an ROI for "Gratefulness", but he includes in that chapter a case study about the Donors Choose organization, and a test they did of sending out thank-you notes to donors ... the study found that those who received the notes ended up being 38% more likely to give again over those who were not specifically thanked (in actual snail-mail notes, not e-mails).

Likeable Business[3] concludes with an interesting analogy ... *when faced with a quick decision, large or small, ask yourself: "Would this be a winning decision at a cocktail party?"* ...

> The person at a cocktail party who listens, who tells great stories, who is responsive, authentic, passionate, and grateful, will be the hit of the party time after time and will derive the most value from the party.

Now, this has been out for over a year, so might not be as widely stocked in the brick-and-mortar book vendors, but its a testament to its popularity that it hasn't dropped deeply in price in the used channels. The on-line guys have it at a bit more than a quarter off of cover, but you'll still be forking out ten bucks with shipping if you go with a used copy. I enjoyed this quite a bit, finding it informative and entertaining in nearly equal parts.

Notes:

1. http://btripp-books.livejournal.com/151272.html
2-3. http://amzn.to/1GhAn4b

Sunday, November 10, 2013[1]

No, really ... there ARE "safe nukes"!

As regular readers know, pretty much every month I get some book or another from the LibraryThing.com "Early Reviewer" program, and, generally speaking, I'm usually content to deal with whatever the "Almighty Algorithm" doles out to me from the books I've requested. However, a month or so back, there was a book that I *didn't* win that I'd really been interested in reading, Richard Martin's SuperFuel: Thorium, the Green Energy Source for the Future[2]. I figured "what the heck?", dug up the contact info for the publishers (the good folks at Macmillan), and shot off an email requesting a review copy, which they kindly provided. So, this represents a slightly new (or something of a "mashup") way of my coming to read a particular title.

I'd been interested in Thorium since reading about "4th generation" reactors in Peter Diamandis' Abundance[3], and was particularly interested in the "green energy" angle for my Green Tech Chicago[4] blog, so I was quite eager to jump into reading this.

The author is a noted science writer, with credits in a number of high-profile publications, as well as being the "editorial director" of a research firm[5] *that provides in-depth analysis of global clean technology markets*. While this might have been more involving had it been penned by one of the individuals actually engaged in Thorium development, his research into the subject appears to have been quite expansive (although he didn't seem to have caught wind of the laser/Thorium system that has been recently in the news[6]).

SuperFuel[7] is structured largely on the threads of particular individuals, and their relationships to the development of Thorium as an energy source. It starts with Kirk Sorensen, who Martin had met in 2009 while working on an article for *Wired*. In 2002 Sorensen had encountered a book *Fluid Fuel Reactors* which had totally engaged him in this new area of research ... leading him to begin the Energy from Thorium[8] blog. He is used as a springboard for Martin to introduce *a lot* of technical detail comparing various types of reactors, and in-depth descriptions of several designs that would make use of Thorium, all of which have advantages over current systems. I wish I could grab a particular paragraph in this, but I'd have to pull *pages* on LTFRs (Liquid Fluoride Thorium Reactors) to put the system into context, so here are just a few highlights regarding the reactors and Thorium:

> It is abundant, In fact, used properly, it's effectively inexhaustible. ...
>
> It requires no special refining or processing beyond purifying it from the monazite ore in which it is most commonly found. ...

> It's no good for making weapons. In fact, it's not fissile at all. ...
>
> ... reactors based on thorium ... consume far more of the latent energy trapped inside the fuel, vastly reducing or even eliminating the problem of nuclear waste. ...
>
> Because the core is composed of a molten salt with an extremely high boiling point, it operates at atmospheric pressure ...
>
> LFTRs ... generate fission products {with} half-lives ... measured in dozens of years, not thousands.
>
> LFTRs are impervious to sudden overheating ...
>
> {T}hey can run indefinitely. The reactions in a LFTR produce enough excess neutrons to breed their own fuel. ...
>
> LFTRs are 200 to 300 times more fuel efficient than legacy reactors. They are safer, simpler, smaller, less expensive to build. ...
>
> No rational from-scratch approach to nuclear power would build anything else, yet we are burdened with ... unsafe uranium reactors that produce tons of long-lived nuclear waste. ... How did this happen? Why were thorium-based molten salt reactors abandoned when they showed such promise at the dawn of the atomic age?

That question moves the book to the next set of protagonists, Alvin Weinberg and Hyman Rickover, along with Weinberg's mentor, Eugene Wigner.

Weinberg and Wigner were involved in the Manhattan Project, specifically in the drive to produce Plutonium for the atomic bombs. However, *"Weinberg had come to believe that liquid fuel thorium reactors would transform the nation's energy supply"* and had managed to develop a proof-of-concept installation. Unfortunately, between the race for the bomb (against what was perceived as Germany's program), and the post-war chess game with the Soviets, a system that did not produce bomb-making materials was unwelcome in the military-controlled nuclear niche:

> National defense requirements imposed three basic limitations on Weinberg and the others who sought to develop a peacetime nuclear power base: All scientific data relating to nuclear technology was classified, severely restricting information flow. Innovation in nuclear power was subservient to the maintenance of superiority in the arms race; of premier importance was ensuring a sufficient supply of weapons-grade uranium and plutonium ... Finally, reactor development ... was channeled

> *into programs that would directly benefit military operations – meaning, in the first case, submarine propulsion.*

Which brings in Admiral Rickover, and the ascendency of the pressurized water reactor. The issue that the Navy had with the liquid sodium reactors was that sodium reacts explosively with water and *"the Navy had the best plumbers in the world"* and *"they knew how to design and operate pumps, bearings, and valves to transport water, including water at high pressure required for a nuclear reactor inside a submarine."* So, the now-dominant PWR system became established *"not as a commercial power plant, and not because it was cheap or inherently safer than other reactors, but rather because it ... lent itself to naval propulsion"* despite the U.S. having designs for Molten Salt Reactors using plentiful, and far safer, Thorium as fuel as early as 1959.

How did this get so derailed? Well,

> *The original nuclearati almost all trained at Rickover's feet. Single-handedly he had established the foundation for the nation's civilian and military reactor development. ... His power unchallenged, Rickover set about building a nuclear power industry in his own image. And that was the problem. Rickover's authoritarian style of leadership, his intolerance of dissent, and his valuing of efficiency over creativity and open discussion all bled into the roots of the nuclear power establishment. ... Rickover ... undermined and eliminated potential ... competing nuclear programs ... the field of nuclear engineering is only now recovering from Rickover's single-minded view of the technology.*

While the nuclear power industry in the U.S. is locked into a PWR model, both India and China are rushing ahead to develop Thorium-based nuclear plants. Of course, nuclear power has been a big "scare" item in the Western press, and the fear of all things nuclear has been deeply engrained in the U.S. population ... a situation not improved by Fukushima disaster.

Martin paints a very dire picture (comparing it to the collapse of the Roman Empire) for the U.S. if we don't move forward with Thorium power. In the last part of the book he details what he sees as a necessary action plan for developing fourth-generation reactors based on the LFTR system ... spelling out costs and timelines, all of which seem entirely plausible if we can get past the fears and the institutional intransigence of the current nuclear industry. You can sense the author's frustration in looking at a way of generating power that not only is safe, affordable, and can even clean up the stockpiles of waste from previous plants while producing electricity for the planet essentially *forever*, but which is being ignored, belittled, and demonized in the country that developed it.

If you have an interest in "green energy", or future technology in general, you really should pick up a copy of SuperFuel[9]. Even though this was in the "early reviewers" program, the book has been out (in hardcover) for a while, with the paperback edition new this August. I'm guessing that you should be able to find that "wherever books are sold", but the online big boys have it for a bit under cover (and the new/used guys have new copies for about half off). Obviously, moving to Thorium would make sense for the whole world, but as a species how much sense do we have?

Notes:

1. http://btripp-books.livejournal.com/151347.html

2. http://amzn.to/1FiaW0f

3. http://btripp-books.livejournal.com/128282.html

4. http://www.chicagonow.com/green-tech-chicago

5. http://www.navigantresearch.com/

6. http://www.chicagonow.com/green-tech-chicago/2013/11/wow-and-it-looks-like-the-batmobile/

7. http://amzn.to/1FiaW0f

8. http://energyfromthorium.com/

9. http://amzn.to/1FiaW0f

Sunday, December 1, 2013[1]

And in this corner ...

I've been quite a fan of Gary Vaynerchuk's previous books, Crush It![2] and The Thank You Economy[3], both of which I felt were "game changing" and major "philosophical" statements about the social media field, and how that has been driving an evolution of business models in general. As I noted in my previous reviews, Gary isn't some academic sitting on the sidelines and pontificating on what's what, he's been building businesses down on the street, first taking his family's liquor store and creating a significant on-line wine distribution organization from it (largely on the back of his web videos), and, more recently, creating his own social/digital agency to put into practice what he's been preaching beyond the wine world.

So, when I requested a review copy of his new Jab, Jab, Jab, Right Hook: How to Tell Your Story in a Noisy Social World[4] from the good folks at Harper Collins' Harper Business imprint, I was sort of expecting the same sort of rah-rah, get out there and change the world, inspirational vibe that I'd gotten from the previous titles. And I was initially disappointed that this book was *not* "vol 3" of what Gary had put out previously. This was not the football halftime talk to get the team battle-ready, but something else ... more tactical, more specific.

As one can get from the cover/title, the central analogy at work here is social media as boxing, where one works one opponent (here, slightly uncomfortably, one's audience) with a series of "targeted jabs" before trying to land that big right hook. The tone here is Gary leaning into the ring to talk to his fighter (the company) and telling them to land a few dozen body blows and other "jabs" ... very technical, very nuanced, and very platform-specific. And, frankly, I kept waiting for it to get to the big stadium rock anthem level, and was disappointed when it wasn't "going there". However, at one point the light went on, and I started to "get" what Gary was doing here ... which, again, is very different from his previous books.

The first sixth of the book discusses the broad strokes of how the messages of the previous books have come across, and setting up the focus of this one ... I think this bit puts it into a good framework (although that ellipsis I put in the following represents a gap of about half a page):

> Marketers are constantly asking me for a fixed storytelling blueprint, something that delineates the optimal number of jabs before it's appropriate to throw a right hook. That blueprint doesn't exist. Social media storytelling is as sweet a science as boxing, requiring constant experimentation and hours of observation. ...A fighter will concentrate on trying to hit his opponent's body if he learns that the competitor is reluctant to get hit there. But

> *the next guy he fights might not be afraid to get hit in the body, so he'll have to change his approach.*
>
> *Similarly, each platform is unique, and requires a unique formula. What works on Facebook won't necessarily work on Twitter. Stories told through pictures on Instagram don't resonate the same way when told in an identical manner on Pinterest. Posting the same content on Tumblr as on Google+ is the equivalent of the tourist deciding that since he can't speak Norwegian he'll just speak Icelandic and it will do. That's stupid. Both languages share similar roots and are spoken by tall, gorgeous blondes, but aside from that, they're totally different. Today, getting people to hear your story on social media, and then act on it, requires using a platform's native language, paying attention to context, understanding the nuances and subtle differences that make each platform unique, and adapting your content to match.*

He goes on to further focus that advice on mobile, given the ever-increasing importance of the small-screen, and then moves into a section which defines "outstanding content" as that which follows six rules:

1. It's Native
2. It Doesn't Interrupt
3. It Doesn't Make Demands - Often
4. It Leverages Pop Culture
5. It's Micro
6. It's Consistent and Self-Aware

There are some really dramatic side-by-side comparisons in the first section of what is "native" on a platform and what's not. This foreshadows much of the rest of the book, where examples of brands that are doing it right are put up against brands that aren't and the good and the bad picked over with a relatively fine-toothed comb. Oh, and if you want to make Gary happy ... put pictures in your posts and put your logo on your picture ... you get the feeling that his head was exploding over and over here like a animated .gif from *Scanners* over this point!

The bulk of [Jab, Jab, Jab, Right Hook](#)[5] is going platform to platform and looking at things that brands, from small local operations to mega international household names, have posted. There are a few where Gary gives unqualified kudos, but most are picking things apart and giving blow-by-blow "what they should have done" commentary. The chapters go "Storytell on Facebook", "Listen Well on Twitter", "Glam It Up on Pinterest", "Create Art on Instagram", "Get Animated on Tumblr", and then one on "emerging networks" which includes LinkedIn, Google+, Vine (on which Gary's quite active), and Snapchat. Each of the main chapters starts with a history of the platform, when founded, how many users each has, some trivia (like the Twitter bird's name being "Larry"), growth, acquisitions, etc., then moving into an over-view essay on how the platform "works" within the social media universe, before going into the specific examples where he pulls apart large numbers of items, discusses what right/wrong with them, and then offers up general statements, with a closing "list" of "Questions To Ask About Your [platform] Content". Most of the advice here is pretty specific, such as this for Instagram:

> Go crazy with your hashtags: Hashtags matter here, maybe even more than they do on Twitter. In Twitter, the hashtag can sometimes be the sprinkle – a dash of irony, a smattering of humor that you use once, maybe twice per day. On Instagram, hastags are the whole darn cupcake. You can't overuse them. Putting out five, six, or even ten hashtags in a row per post isn't a bad way to communicate.

The book closes with a few summarizing chapters (and one added at the last minute when Instagram introduced its videos), which tie back into the boxing analogy and the suggestion that

> "Content is King, Context is God, and then there's effort ... without effort – intense, consistent, committed, 24-7 effort – the best social media micro-content placed within the most appropriate will go down as gracelessly as {Douglas losing to Holyfield}".

Once I "got" the level at which Jab, Jab, Jab, Right Hook[6] was operating, I quite enjoyed it ... it is incredibly detailed, and picks apart existing campaigns so that the reader can avoid making the same mistakes. Picking up this book is like hiring a top-notch coach to be sitting in your corner, in this case Gary Vaynerchuk telling you to punch here and not there, when to go for the jaw and when to duck. This is brand new, just being officially released this week, so it should be coming through your local brick-and-mortar book vendors with business/marketing sections in a big way right about now, but the online big boys have it at a very generous 40% off of cover at the moment. I was surprised to have gotten a hardcover edition of the book, following up on the ARC edition I'd initially been sent, but I think Harper made a good call on it, as the "finished" book is far more impressive, with full color photography and high quality paper throughout, making it evident that the book's quite a good deal, even at full cover price! I can't imagine anybody doing any level of marketing in the social media sphere *not* getting a solid benefit from this book ... it's sort of the "practical workbook" to put in place the "philosophical" calls to action in Vaynerchuk's previous books.

Notes:

1. http://btripp-books.livejournal.com/151726.html
2. http://btripp-books.livejournal.com/88717.html
3. http://btripp-books.livejournal.com/107420.html
4-6. http://amzn.to/1Ed0x22

Saturday, December 28, 2013[1]

Where work is heading?

When I requested this book from the good folks at Random House's "Crown Business" imprint, I didn't know just how immediate the subject was going to be for me. As long-term readers of my main blog space (from where these reviews originate before cloning off into other zones on the web) will realize, I've worked from home in various roles for 17 of the past 20 years. However, a couple of months back, I got hired on a contract to do writing for a company out in "the land beyond O'Hare", and was suddenly on the flipside of this dynamic, facing a 2.5 hour commute each way (that full-time contract has since been shifted to about a half-time freelancing gig, which, while bringing in a good deal less money, also doesn't suck 25 hours/week into time spent on various buses and trains). It was largely during those commutes that I ended up reading Jason Fried & David Heinemeier Hansson's (the founders of 37Signals) new book, Remote: Office Not Required[2] ... somewhat ironic timing.

Remote[3], like Fried and Hansson's previous ReWork[4], is a quick read, in that a substantial percentage (a third?) of its 250 pages are pictures ... either illustrating points in the text or riffing off on related concepts. The authors are dedicated advocates for remote work, having built their software company up out of a collection of workers in various locations around the world, with only about a half of their staff at their Chicago headquarters. They note in the opening that between 2005 and 2011 the number of U.S. Remote workers increased 73% - although the total number is still a rather slim 3 million. They also cite the "firestorm" on the subject sparked by Yahoo!'s Marissa Mayer who earlier this year canceled all remote work arrangements that company was offering.

Now, it would be easy to point at companies like 37Signals and say that remote work was just for cutting-edge software makers and the like, but one of the leading lights of this movement is staid, no-nonsense, established old IBM. My wife's BFF's husband has been an IBM lifer, and he got sent home with a laptop, a high-speed internet connection, and a budget for setting up a home office *nearly 20 years ago* ... so this isn't just a recent "flash in the pan" approach.

And, it's not just tech sector companies ... Aetna has nearly half of its employees working from home ... Deloitte has 86% of its people working remotely at least 20% of the time ... in government, 85% of the examiners for the U.S. Patent & Trademark Office, 57% of NASA's workers, and 67% of the E.P.A.'s employees work remotely to some extent ... and, back in tech, Intel lets 82% of their people regularly work remotely. IBM did a white paper on the subject, "Working Outside the Box"[5], from which a lot of the facts and figures here are drawn.

Most of the book is directed to business owners, as there is a lot about hiring, collaborating, etc., even though there are sections "coaching" workers on how to best manage working remotely. One of the early pitches they make here, in the section on how unhealthy commuting is, really stood out to me:

> But let's say we ignore the overwhelming evidence that commuting doesn't do a body good. Pretend it isn't bad for the environment either. Let's just do the math. Say you spend thirty minutes driving in rush hour every morning and another fifteen getting to your car and into the office. That's 1.5 hours a day, 7.5 hours per week, or somewhere between 300 and 400 hours per year, give or take holidays and vacation. Four hundred hours is exactly the amount of programmer time we spent building Basecamp, our most popular product. Imagine what you could do with 400 extra hours a year. Commuting isn't just bad for you, your relationships, and the environment – it's bad for business. And it doesn't have to be that way.

In the introductory material they say that they really wished that Marissa Mayer had held off about six months before releasing her dictate about remote working (as sales of Remote[6] would have greatly benefited!), and point out that nearly *all* the discussion that happened in the wake of that is reflected in the "Dealing With Excuses" chapter.

One thing I found *fascinating* here is that the authors only ask 40 hours a week from their employees ... saying *"There are no hero awards for putting in more than that."* (as a regular thing). Having myself worked (in my publishing days) 14 hours a day, 7 days a week, I know just how the "hero" thing can get a hold on your key workers. They address this here:

> It starts innocently enough. You wake up by opening your laptop in bed and answering a few emails from last night. ... Before you know it, you've stretched the workday from 7am to 9pm.
>
> That's the great irony of letting passionate people work from home. A manager's natural instinct is to worry about his workers not getting enough work done, but the real threat is that <u>too</u> much will likely get done. And because the manager isn't sitting across from his worker anymore, he can't look into the person's eyes and see burnout.

At 37Signals, their rule-of-thumb is the idea of "a good day's work" ... the employee should be able to ask themselves if they've managed that and come up with an affirmative most days.

Of course, remote working opens up its own challenges ... home workers get far fewer opportunities to get exercise. I know this from personal experience ... over the past five years when I'd been trying to piece together some money from freelance and consulting gigs (while looking for full-time work), I'd be spending 12-18 hours a day at the keyboard, and would only *rarely* come close the recommended 10,000 steps a day (which I track with a Fitbit) since I would go *days* without even leaving the apartment. To combat this, 37Signals provides its workers with a monthly stipend for a health club membership, plus a program called "37 Vegetables"[7] which provides a CSA (Community Supported Agriculture) share for each employee.

Again, one of the most appealing aspects of Remote[8] is that Fried & Hansson have been *doing* this stuff for years, and so the suggestions, guidance, and coaching in here aren't "ivory tower" pronouncements from *theorists*, but down-in-the-trenches experiences of what works and what's likely to be a problem with running (or participating in) a remote work force.

As this came out just last month, it should certainly be out in the brick-and-mortar book vendors that handle business titles ... and the online big boys have it for nearly 40% off of cover. Needless to say, I'm hoping that this manifesto will get traction and more companies take a serious look at the remote work option. I don't think this is as groundbreaking as *ReWork*, but if you have an interest in what might well be "the future of work", do pick up a copy!

Notes:

1. http://btripp-books.livejournal.com/151866.html
2-3. http://amzn.to/1dboy4I
4. http://btripp-books.livejournal.com/98114.html
5. http://www-01.ibm.com/industries/government/ieg/pdf/working_outside_the_box.pdf
6. http://amzn.to/1dboy4I
7. http://37signals.com/svn/posts/3151
8. http://amzn.to/1dboy4I

QR code links to the on-line reviews:

Savage Anxieties:
The Invention of Western Civilization
by
Robert A. Williams, Jr.

The Devil's Dictionary
by
Ambrose Bierce

A Writer's People: Ways of Looking and Feeling
by
V.S. Naipaul

Antifragile: Things that Gain from Disorder
by
Nassim Nicholas Taleb

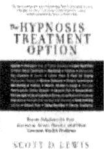

The Hypnosis Treatment Option
by
Scott D. Lewis

The Nazi Séance: The Strange Story
of the Jewish Psychic in Hitler's Circle
by
Arthur J. Magida

Think Like Zuck:
The Five Business Secrets of Facebook's
Improbably Brilliant CEO Mark Zuckerberg
by
Ekaterina Walter

Pinterest Power: Market Your Business,
Sell Your Product, and Build Your Brand
on the World's Hottest Social Network
by
Jason Miles & Karen Lacey

The Fusion Marketing Bible:
Fuse Traditional Media, Social Media,
& Digital Media to Maximize Marketing
by
Lon Safko

Meatball Sundae: Is Your Marketing Out of Sync?
by
Seth Godin

Starting Over: Why the Last Decade
Was so Damn Rotten and Why the Next One
Will Surely Be Better
by
Andy Serwer

The Mesh: Why the Future of Business Is Sharing
by
Lisa Gansky

HTML5 For Dummies Quick Reference
by
Andy Harris

Relentless Innovation: What Works, What Doesn't
– And What That Means For Your Business
by
Jeffrey Phillips

Life's Golden Ticket
by
Brendon Burchard

Let Go To Grow: Why Some Businesses Thrive
and Others Fail to Reach Their Potential
by
Doug and Polly White

Skyscraper Facades of the Gilded Age:
Fifty-One Extravagant Designs, 1875-1910
by
Joseph J. Korom, Jr.

The Seven Wisdoms of Life:
a Journey into the Chakras
by
Shai Tubali

Youtility:
Why Smart Marketing Is about Help Not Hype
by
Jay Baer

China's Great Train: Beijing's Drive West
and the Campaign to Remake Tibet
by
Abrahm Lustgarten

My Path Leads to Tibet: The Inspiring Story
of How One Young Blind Woman Brought Hope
to the Blind Children of Tibet
by
Sabriye Tenberken

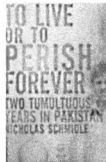

To Live or to Perish Forever:
Two Tumultuous Years in Pakistan
by
Nicholas Schmidle

Exchanges Within: Questions from Everyday Life
by
John Pentland

The Sense of Being Stared At:
And Other Aspects of the Extended Mind
by
Rupert Sheldrake

The Quark and the Jaguar:
Adventures in the Simple and the Complex
by
Murray Gell-Mann

Miraculous Health: How to Heal Your Body
by Unleashing the Hidden Power of Your Mind
by
Dr. Rick Levy

The Alchemist
by
Paulo Coelho

Promote Yourself:
The New Rules for Career Success
by
Dan Schawbel

From the Ground Up:
A Food Grower's Education in Life, Love,
and the Movement That's Changing the Nation
by
Jeanne Nolan

Stop Talking, Start Communicating:
Play Dumb, Be Boring, Blow Things Off, Lose
Your Friends, and Other Counterintuitive Secrets
to Success in Business and in Life
by
Geoffrey Tumlin

Rock & Roll Jihad:
A Muslim Rock Star's Revolution
by
Salman Ahmad

Fabricated: The New World of 3D Printing
by
Hod Lipson & Melba Kurman

Marketing in the Round:
How to Develop an Integrated
Marketing Campaign in the Digital Era
by
Gini Dietrich & Geoff Livingston

QR Codes Kill Kittens:
How to Alienate Customers, Dishearten Employees,
and Drive Your Business into the Ground
by
Scott Stratten

Manuscript Found in Accra
by
Paulo Coelho

The Human Voice: How This Extraordinary Instrument
Reveals Essential Clues About Who We Are
by
Anne Karpf

American on Purpose: The Improbable Adventures of an Unlikely Patriot
by
Craig Ferguson

Permanent Emergency: Inside the TSA and the Fight for the Future of American Security
by
Kip Hawley and Nathan Means

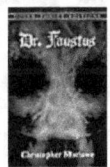

Dr. Faustus
by
Christopher Marlow

Likeable Business: Why Today's Consumers Demand More and How Leaders Can Deliver
by
Dave Kerpen

SuperFuel: Thorium,
the Green Energy Source for the Future
by
Richard Martin

Jab, Jab, Jab, Right Hook:
How to Tell Your Story in a Noisy Social World
by
Gary Vaynerchuk

Remote: Office Not Required
by
Jason Fried & David Heinemeier Hansson

CONTENTS - ALPHABETICAL BY AUTHOR

Salman Ahmad   page 90
Rock & Roll Jihad

Jay Baer   page 54
Youtility

Ambrose Bierce   page 5
The Devil's Dictionary

Brendon Burchard   page 41
Life's Golden Ticket

Paulo Coelho   page 100
Manuscript Found in Accra

Paulo Coelho   page 79
The Alchemist

Gini Dietrich & Geoff Livingston   page 96
Marketing in the Round

Craig Ferguson   page 106
American on Purpose

Jason Fried & David Heinemeier Hansson   page 124
Remote

Lisa Gansky   page 33
The Mesh

Murray Gell-Mann   page 73
The Quark and the Jaguar

Seth Godin   page 28
Meatball Sundae

Andy Harris   page 36
HTML5 For Dummies Quick Reference

Kip Hawley &. Nathan Means   page 108
Permanent Emergency

Anne Karpf   page 103
The Human Voice

Author	Title	Page
Dave Kerpen	Likeable Business	114
Joseph J. Korom, Jr.	Skyscraper Facades of the Gilded Age	47
Dr. Rick Levy	Miraculous Health	76
Scott D. Lewis	The Hypnosis Treatment Option	15
Hod Lipson & Melba Kurman	Fabricated	93
Abrahm Lustgarten	China's Great Train	58
Arthur J. Magida	The Nazi Séance	17
Christopher Marlow	Dr. Faustus	111
Richard Martin	SuperFuel	117
Jason Miles & Karen Lacey	Pinterest Power	22
V.S. Naipaul	A Writer's People	8
Jeanne Nolan	From the Ground Up	84
John Pentland	Exchanges Within	66
Jeffrey Phillips	Relentless Innovation	38
Lon Safko	The Fusion Marketing Bible	25
Dan Schawbel	Promote Yourself	81

Author	Title	Page
Nicholas Schmidle	To Live or to Perish Forever	63
Andy Serwer	Starting Over	31
Rupert Sheldrake	The Sense of Being Stared At	69
Scott Stratten	QR Codes Kill Kittens	98
Nassim Nicholas Taleb	Antifragile	12
Sabriye Tenberken	My Path Leads to Tibet	61
Shai Tubali	The Seven Wisdoms of Life	51
Geoffrey Tumlin	Stop Talking, Start Communicating	87
Gary Vaynerchuk	Jab, Jab, Jab, Right Hook	121
Ekaterina Walter	Think Like Zuck	19
Doug White & Polly White	Let Go To Grow	44
Robert A. Williams, Jr.	Savage Anxieties	1

CONTENTS - ALPHABETICAL BY TITLE

Paulo Coelho	*The Alchemist*	page	79
Craig Ferguson	*American on Purpose*	page	106
Nassim Nicholas Taleb	*Antifragile*	page	12
Abrahm Lustgarten	*China's Great Train*	page	58
Ambrose Bierce	*The Devil's Dictionary*	page	5
Christopher Marlow	*Dr. Faustus*	page	111
John Pentland	*Exchanges Within*	page	66
Hod Lipson & Melba Kurman	*Fabricated*	page	93
Jeanne Nolan	*From the Ground Up*	page	84
Lon Safko	*The Fusion Marketing Bible*	page	25
Anne Karpf	*The Human Voice*	page	103
Andy Harris	*HTML5 For Dummies Quick Reference*	page	36
Scott D. Lewis	*The Hypnosis Treatment Option*	page	15
Gary Vaynerchuk	*Jab, Jab, Jab, Right Hook*	page	121
Doug White & Polly White	*Let Go To Grow*	page	44

Life's Golden Ticket Brendon Burchard	page	41
Likeable Business Dave Kerpen	page	114
Manuscript Found in Accra Paulo Coelho	page	100
Marketing in the Round Gini Dietrich & Geoff Livingston	page	96
Meatball Sundae Seth Godin	page	28
The Mesh Lisa Gansky	page	33
Miraculous Health Dr. Rick Levy	page	76
My Path Leads to Tibet Sabriye Tenberken	page	61
The Nazi Séance Arthur J. Magida	page	17
Permanent Emergency Kip Hawley &.Nathan Means	page	108
Pinterest Power Jason Miles & Karen Lacey	page	22
Promote Yourself Dan Schawbel	page	81
QR Codes Kill Kittens Scott Stratten	page	98
The Quark and the Jaguar Murray Gell-Mann	page	73
Relentless Innovation Jeffrey Phillips	page	38
Remote Jason Fried & David Heinemeier Hansson	page	124

Salman Ahmad	*Rock & Roll Jihad*	page	90
Robert A. Williams, Jr.	*Savage Anxieties*	page	1
Rupert Sheldrake	*The Sense of Being Stared At*	page	69
Shai Tubali	*The Seven Wisdoms of Life*	page	51
Joseph J. Korom, Jr.	*Skyscraper Facades of the Gilded Age*	page	47
Andy Serwer	*Starting Over*	page	31
Geoffrey Tumlin	*Stop Talking, Start Communicating*	page	87
Richard Martin	*SuperFuel*	page	117
Ekaterina Walter	*Think Like Zuck*	page	19
Nicholas Schmidle	*To Live or to Perish Forever*	page	63
V.S. Naipaul	*A Writer's People*	page	8
Jay Baer	*Youtility*	page	54

www.ingramcontent.com/pod-product-compliance
Lightning Source LLC
Chambersburg PA
CBHW070452100426
42743CB00010B/1591